LET'S TALK ABOUT MONEY

The no-nonsense guide
to managing and maximising
your financial independence

Harry Torrance

Let's Talk About Money
ISBN 978-1-915483-35-5 (paperback)
eISBN 978-1-915483-36-2

Published in 2024 by Right Book Press
Printed in the UK

A CIP record of this book is available from the British Library.

Contents

Foreword

By Sarah Megginson, personal finance expert, media commentator and columnist

Harry says he was lucky enough to be able to 'retire at 50', but there's really nothing lucky about it. His financial success didn't happen in a vacuum – there was strategy, commitment, sacrifice and follow-through, all essential ingredients to reach his goal.

And what a goal it was! Retiring from the rat race with enough wealth and health to actually enjoy yourself – well, that's the dream, isn't it? What I love about Harry and his approach to financial freedom is that he's (quite literally) an open book. It's full of practical, real-world advice and it's achievable, without being very heavy on the maths. He's happy to share his secrets and strategies and show you what's actually possible for you, too.

He lays it all out in plain English, which is powerful. The words and the language we use are so very important. Just this week, for instance, I was reading an article in a respected financial newspaper that outlined a wealth creation strategy for a healthy retirement. The article cited two example incomes – both six figures. It mentioned that by taking advantage of a clever tax technique, you could boost your retirement fund 'while taking only a £2,975 hit to your annual take-home pay'. Only? You're in a special band of income when almost £3,000 is considered 'only' a small amount!

For many people, a sum far smaller than this can be

make or break. For them, the idea of giving up hundreds of pounds each month in your take-home pay – even if sacrificing £3,000 now means a significantly wealthier future – is a pure impossibility. So, the advice offered in that article was designed for the fortunate few who earn high incomes.

That's often how it goes with wealth planning and with money conversations in general; it's inaccessible to everyday people. Paying for financial planning advice is expensive, and people can gatekeep the secrets to their own success – sometimes because they don't want to share, but more often because money is so taboo to talk about.

That's the really powerful thing about Harry's journey. He's starting a conversation and showing you what's possible. Importantly, he's demonstrating that what he did (and I mean this with utmost respect) wasn't special. In his own words, it was ordinary, and Harry believes virtually anyone can achieve a similar outcome.

You might have to challenge some of your long-held beliefs. You may have to look at things a little differently. But in reading this book, you'll gain a good, basic understanding of personal finance, alongside the tools and strategies you need to work towards a more financially secure future.

Harry and his wife are simply a regular couple who've done it: they've lived and learned that the secret to financial success is to spend less than you earn, and invest the rest wisely. And now, you can too.

Sarah Megginson brings over two decades of experience in property and finance journalism to her role as a personal finance expert with global financial comparison site Finder. A mother of three, Sarah is deeply committed to educating the next generation on earning, investing and managing money effectively. www.sarahmegginson.com

Prologue

Alex, 28 (friend and former colleague)

On a chilly December night back in 2018, I stepped into the bustling world of Amazon as a fresh-faced graduate. There, in Stoke-on-Trent, England, I found myself as the night shift manager, a role that felt dauntingly grand for my novice shoulders. It was in those early days (well, nights) that I first met Harry, not just a colleague but soon to become a mentor and a friend, perceptive enough to see my hesitations without me uttering a word. With a mix of humour and wisdom, he urged me to embrace the challenge, saying, 'This is your new playground – go be a cowboy.' It was the encouragement I needed to transform trepidation into determination.

Our relationship evolved over the years, filled with countless conversations about work, life, and aspirations. Harry, with his unique blend of realism and ambition, shared his personal goal of retiring early – a dream that deeply resonated with me. When he announced his retirement at the ripe old age of 52, I was both amazed and inspired. Probing him for tips, I found no shortcuts or easy paths. Instead, he offered honest, hard-earned insights.

Guided by our conversations, I started to carve my own path. Today, as I write this from Sydney, Australia, poised to invest in my second property, I realise how Harry's mentorship has been instrumental in shaping my journey. He didn't just help me devise a plan for my career, finances and personal life, he instilled in me the confidence to pursue it.

Now, as Harry turns his wealth of experience and insights into the pages of this book, I feel privileged to pen this prologue as a taster of what you can achieve. For those about to embark on this read, you're in for a treat. His pragmatic wisdom, peppered with his (often) quirky view of life, is not just enlightening but also deeply relatable. It's a guide from someone who's walked the path and is generous enough to share the map.

Happy reading, and may you find your own way to 'be a cowboy' in your life's endeavours, just as Harry inspired me to do in mine.

Introduction

In March 2022, a few months after my wife Lou had stopped working full time, I did the same. Since then, I've taken on a couple of (very) short-term contracting jobs but otherwise we have effectively 'retired' – and we're both in our mid-fifties. We have a financial plan that allows us to spend our time doing pretty much exactly what we want. I'm reaping the benefits of that new life: I'm sleeping better, eating more healthily, taking more exercise, have lost a stone in weight over the course of a year and rarely get stressed, least of all about money.

Sounds great, doesn't it? Well, it is – but that's not the point of this book. As we got closer to leaving our jobs and sharing our plans with others, the most common question was 'How?' And there were lots of variations, including: 'How did you do it?', 'How do you know you have enough money?' and 'How did you start?' As I started explaining it to friends and colleagues, it dawned on me that there were many different elements to our plan, several common themes, and it's been a long time in the planning. This also fed into a passion of mine for mentoring and how I could share our approach with other people so that they too might have a more secure financial plan, which in turn could lead to a more comfortable life.

But let's be clear, there's no quick fix or shortcut and some of the choices are hard, particularly when your long-held beliefs are challenged. And I'm not going to promise that you can replicate our plan to the letter and simply 'retire at 50'. Why? Because everyone is different

1

and we all have different aspirations, situations, skills and hobbies. However, I can walk you through the approach to life and finance that allowed us to achieve this and would argue that you can apply many of the techniques in this book and build your own plan to a more secure financial future. I can also guarantee you that these approaches are 'real world achievable'; in researching this book, I've read countless articles for background information and trawled the internet for similar content, each time sense-checking that what I'm saying holds water.

One popular blog had a little gem hidden in a post: 'My wife and I moved state and changed jobs, doubling our salaries.' Really? This is fantasy-land for most people and totally unrealistic. Just to set the record straight, I've not had a pay rise for probably half the years I've worked and when I have it's generally been in the low single digits as a percentage. I've had some step-changes in salary when changing jobs but nowhere near double. Also, much of this internet-based content is US-centric and the fiscal examples aren't applicable over here, so that's another reason why I wanted to write this book – specifically to target a local audience.

As I write, here in the UK we're in the middle of some challenging economic times. We've come through the Covid-19 pandemic but many businesses haven't fully recovered; the war in Ukraine continues, contributing to higher fuel and food prices; we have experienced stubborn inflation and have had a pretty unstable government throughout. This has hit everyone hard. Research from insurance group Direct Line in January 2023 suggested that almost a third (32%) have stopped adding to their savings due to the rising cost of living, a quarter of households (25%) don't have any savings at all, and more than a fifth (22%) of households wouldn't last a month before getting into financial difficulties if the main breadwinner was unable to work.

Researching and writing this book has taken about two years, so it certainly isn't a knee-jerk reaction to the cost of living crisis or about making a quick buck. As I've said before, there are very few quick wins and it takes time, but even in these circumstances I can explain some tools and approaches for you to build a plan to make your future more financially secure. I think it's fair to say that many people are simply not very good at managing their finances and they're not very good at admitting it either. If this sounds a little like you, then that's OK – I want to help. The good news is that you don't have to be great at maths to follow the methods in this book; you just need to understand the basic principles of finance and how to make financial decisions that are right for you.

I hated maths at school and wasn't particularly good at it – I struggled to get a 'D' at A-level and only then because it was a requirement for an engineering degree. So rest assured that this isn't going to be a textbook full of number crunching; I'll just show you some examples to help you understand the principles. This is partly because I'm still no good at maths – if you asked me on the spot to work out the compound interest at 5% on £10,000 over 10 years I probably couldn't but I know the effect is good and when it would be applicable to your finances.

The final aspect of this 'knowledge gap' is that not only are many people not very good at admitting they don't understand their finances, they're also slightly embarrassed and therefore don't talk about it. You might be one of these people. I don't care who you talk to – your mum, your partner, your friends or your kids – but not talking about it perpetuates the myth that it's hugely difficult, meaning you might bury your head in the sand rather than try to figure it out. How many times have you been chatting to someone who's just bought a new car on finance and somewhere in the conversation you'll hear the line 'Oh yeah, I got a really great deal', without them knowing whether 3% over five years with a 20% deposit would have been better than 4% over three years with a 25% deposit? I couldn't tell you off the top of my head which is better either, but I can explain how to approach that discussion before signing the deal and which questions to ask so that you'll be more comfortable that you've got the deal that works for you.

A good tool to benchmark your approach to money, or determine your 'financial personality', is one developed by the Myers-Briggs Company and Goldman Sachs. It's a free, ten-question online quiz (see the link in the Resources section at the end of the book) and is a great starting point to better understand your relationship with finance and how you make financial decisions. Irrespective of the result, it will ask the sort of probing questions that will help you start to understand your relationship with money and finances.

I'd like to say that this book is aimed at everyone as we all have to manage our money, but there's a time in your life when money or finances begin to have a greater impact and you start to feel a little out of your depth or don't have the confidence to share that you're not fully in control. This might be when you start your first job, when you move away from home or when you start a family – but it's certainly that point when you realise you have to take financial decisions seriously. You could be in your twenties, thirties or even forties but you'll have started making bigger and more important financial decisions. If you're under 20, even better, as the longer you have, the more effective your plan will be. Don't worry about when you start, as long as you start – and today is as good a day as any. There's an old Chinese proverb which demonstrates this point:

When is the best time to plant a tree? Twenty years ago.
When is the second best time to plant a tree? Today.

Talking of time frames, I grew up in the 1970s and 1980s when life was very different. When I was at school, we had one phone and it was attached to the wall with a curly cable. Our information was sourced from books in the library and we only had four TV channels (and they stopped broadcasting at midnight). Only cameras took photographs and you had to wait until you'd taken 24 or 36 before sending the film away for a week to be printed. Since then, I've seen the birth of home computers, laptops, digital cameras, mobiles, smartphones, email and the internet, and the rise and fall of video, then CDs. Set against these technological advances is the way finance has developed. First, the general principles of economics have stayed the same: companies make things, buy and sell or provide a service and create a profit by increasing their customer base or margin. As they grow, so a company's value increases. Although what they make or sell or how they deliver that service has changed dramatically with technology, the way those companies are valued is the same, and that provides a stable base for a long-term financial plan. Where technology, in my view, has destabilised personal finance is in the range and availability of credit (of the 'buy now, pay later' variety), the complexity of financial products (such as cryptocurrencies or the way debt can be packaged, restructured and sold to another institution, several times over) and the ability to create duplicate (or copycat) products that look and feel like a well-known item but are cheaper and lower quality. These all contribute to a society where many things are proportionally cheaper and more readily available, leading to a risk of spending your money more freely than we did 10 or 20 years ago.

The reason for mentioning this bit of history is that it has influenced much of the way I think and formed the basis of my approach to finance. There was no online marketplace, next-day delivery or instant download of the latest film; if you couldn't afford it, you had to save up for it, and if it wasn't available in your local shop, you had to wait 28 days for delivery, if you could get it delivered at all. Don't get me wrong; I love the current world we live in, with all the benefits technology and progress have brought, but the mindset of waiting and thinking about a purchase and valuing that purchase is, to my mind, quite different to that of many today. This understanding of how we think about spending the money we have is half of the plan, the other half being how to earn more in the first place.

In this book, I'll be covering the key principles of financial planning, together with an overview of the different types of finance and investment. I promise this won't be too technical but it will show you how to evaluate the true benefit (to you) of a financial decision and how to differentiate between several competing options. Then I'll dive into linked concepts of spending less and earning more. This is where you'll be challenged to put in some effort, as failing to grasp these two things can seriously damage your plan. The next section will be on marketing, value and debunking some 'get rich quick' schemes, as it's important to understand that very few businesses are 'on your side' – they exist to make money out of you. But there are also several eye openers that can help reduce your spending. I'll also talk about relationships – many of you will be in them but unfortunately they don't all end 'happily ever after'. However, now's the time to stand up and take ownership of how you're going to manage yourself and your finances, whether it's on your own, as a couple or as a family. Don't worry too much about your starting point – the plan is adaptable. As long as you understand the basics, you can build one that works for you.

And finally, I'm sorry to tell you but, at some point, you're going to die. It's an often overlooked aspect of financial planning and one that people only start thinking about in their sixties or seventies – and that's too late. So let's put it on the table and build it into your plan from the start. To finish, I'll cover how to monitor your plan and ensure that you keep tabs on whether or not you're on track. Again, this won't be too complicated – it involves a bit of spreadsheet work and some examples of some of the technology that makes this bit even easier. If you do want more detail, turn to the Resources section at the back of the book. So grab yourself a cup of tea and start learning how to unravel the mysteries of personal finance, taking those first steps towards creating a plan that will increase your money confidence and give you financial freedom.

Chapter 1

My background and worldview

My wife and I fund our lifestyle through our savings, property and pension investments, which we've built up over the long term but consolidated into an early retirement plan over the past ten years. It's not strictly true that we've given up work altogether; it's more accurate to say that we've given up paid work as we volunteer with a number of local charitable organisations. This was always part of the plan – to give something back to society while having the freedom to do what we want the rest of the time. Yes, we have been and still are frugal but we'll also spend money on having fun. For example, last year we bought a BMW Z4 convertible and have booked first-class flights to Barbados in the spring. But the car is a ten-year-old model bought at auction and 80% of the cost of the flights was covered by points built up on a credit card over the past four years. It's really about the mindset you have about money and financial decision making, how you value what you buy and how you think about long-term saving. That's been a key part of what we've done. It's the confidence we have in making those decisions that allows us to be stress free about the way we live now.

We haven't won the lottery, neither have we inherited a fortune. Although my parents have died and left me a small inheritance, that was never part of the plan. We always intended to fund our lifestyle ourselves. We haven't enjoyed huge salaries or bonuses and, although we've both been in near continual employment, many of our friends have been (and some still are) earning more than we ever did. However, we have enjoyed good health and had a few lucky breaks along the way, some of which were of our making, some of which were just the way the cards were dealt. Similarly, it's not all been plain sailing – I've been made redundant and we've had periods out of work, I've had credit card debts, and we've suffered crippling mortgage payments. If anything, these strengthened our resolve to be financially secure and prove that even when times are tough you can survive.

My story so far

I've had a stable family background and a good education. I'm forever grateful to my parents for making the sacrifices necessary for me to go to private school and, while I wasn't a particularly brilliant pupil, it did instil in me a work ethic and acceptance of discipline and structure that have helped me throughout my life. It was also what prompted me to go to university, mainly because everyone else did. I have an enquiring mind, I'm practical and believe I have a lot of common sense. I've got where I am by working hard and the fact that I twigged early in life that I needed some form of financial game plan, first to get me out of debt and second to secure my financial future. It's become integral to my mindset in thinking about finances, which has developed into a tenacity to be able to stick to that plan.

I left university with a degree in Production Engineering and Manufacturing Management but probably the most important life skill I came away with was learning how to cook on a budget! However, this didn't help me find a job – I graduated just as the country was coming out of a recession in the early 1990s. My dad had taken on a small printing franchise, so I worked for him for a few years. As much as I loved the creativity and wanted to take on the business, he was insistent that I forged my own way in life, so I continued applying for graduate jobs and finally landed a role with a partnership between Warwick University and a wheel manufacturing company.

I started out as an engineer working on a novel project to get computer screens onto the shop floor (effectively an early version of an intranet). I stayed on after the project ended and took over management of the IT system. During my time there I was mentored by the technical director, who taught me about Japanese production efficiency through the likes of Dr W Edwards Deming and his 14 principles, and Japanese industrial engineer Shigeo Shingo. What I saw was that the application of common sense and a simple approach to problem solving could translate outside the world of the production line, and I've used these principles throughout my career. It was also here that I met Lou, and we married in 2003. She ran the tyre distribution operation in the North and I was based in the Midlands, so it prompted us to move jobs and relocate a little further south, working for a European distribution company. I worked there as the IT manager, expanding into quality, and through merger and acquisition ended up closing the site in the south and commuting to Scotland as operations manager for a number of years. Again, the UK was in recession (2008/9) and we felt it was better to have a job than not, so we had a couple of years of remote living before I took redundancy. After about a year, I secured a project manager role with a parcel company before I was enticed to join Amazon as part of their fledgling logistics team. I stayed there for just under eight years before finally deciding we could achieve our plan of early retirement.

It hasn't been a particularly structured career in terms of a long-term plan but at each change of job, there was a progression or step up, leading to a wide variety of roles and locations. I had some excellent mentors along the way, who were instrumental in shaping the way I think about business and, by extension, finance. For the most part, I've enjoyed all my jobs but, like many, I've had my share of working for and with people I didn't particularly gel with. The positive from this was to spur me on to move teams and widen my experience or move company. Throughout my career, there have been a number of times when something has happened to me or I've remembered a conversation that has stuck with me; looking back, these form some pivotal moments in my financial learning.

Pivotal moments

In the sixth form, I remember two general studies classes. One was delivered by an actuary from Norwich Union (now Aviva) who was so boring it made me think I never wanted a career in finance, which is a little ironic, given where I've ended up. The second was delivered by our geography teacher and basically enlightened us about money and budgeting at university. Up to that point, I literally had no idea about student finance, other than the fact that there was a grant. It was my first time living away from home and I hadn't thought about rent, electricity, laundry or food, let alone how there might be any money left over for beer and running a car!

Later, as part of the Warwick University scheme, I was enrolled in the university pension for two years. I knew

I wasn't likely to work in the public sector long term so tried to transfer it into a private pension but at every turn I was told by the scheme's administrators (one of the UK's big four accounting companies) that I couldn't because it made no financial sense to give up the guaranteed benefits I'd receive on retiring. My dad's accountant stepped in to explain that the fund was so small that by the time I retired it wouldn't cover the cost of a daily newspaper and a loaf of bread per week, so it was a shallow argument. It resonated with me that not everyone giving advice is either on your side or has any common sense. It was also around this time that I contracted out of part of the State Pension (through the State Earnings Related Pension Scheme or SERPS – see Green 2023) on the basis that I preferred to be in control of my own pension, rather than relying totally on the government. This early experience of pensions led me to become a pension trustee in a later role, which allowed me to get some first-hand training in how pensions actually work and how large pension funds manage investments. It was an invaluable experience.

Thinking back to my first mentor, he also introduced me to metrics and, more importantly, key metrics. By this I mean a single measure that shows how you're doing, rather than a myriad of tables, graphs and statistics which can be used to 'spin' performance in a better light. He asked me every month to track the number of wheels made and the total labour hours in the factory. Over three years we showed that the 'wheels per labour hour' more than doubled, meaning that our output produced twice as many wheels for the same labour input. Irrespective of which department was contributing to this, overall the factory was 'more efficient'. Again, I've used this approach throughout my life and adapted it to our finances as well, to look for a single, simple measure of how well we're doing.

Long before Chris Tarrant uttered the immortal question 'Who wants to be a millionaire?', the welding shop manager of the wheel company asked me something very similar. When I joined, the company had been through a chequered period, with the previous owners having absconded with the pension fund. There was a new pension scheme in place but understandably the company was overcommunicating at every opportunity to ensure employees felt their investments were safe. In one discussion about how challenging it was for older employees starting from scratch again, this wise old sage commented, 'Don't worry about us, you've got bigger problems – you'll need a pension pot of about a million to have any sort of retirement.' At the time, I was earning £12,000 a year and the thought of building a pension that size was overwhelming and seemed impossible. It was certainly a challenge and while I've not achieved that figure, I'm very close. Because I've chosen to stop working earlier than most, I can't contribute much more but I'm confident I'd have achieved it had I stayed working for longer. However, it does illustrate that what seem like huge goals can be achieved over a long period of time – but you need to actively work towards them. One million probably needs adjusting for inflation but the exact figure is largely irrelevant; it's the fact that it's a big number and when you start it seems an impossibility but it gives you a big, clear target to aim for.

As I've already mentioned, I was lucky enough to have had some excellent mentors early in my career – senior employees who took the time to talk to, encourage and offer advice to younger staff like me. One, who was also my boss, turned down my proposals to upgrade some low-specification computers. I protested, to which he said, 'You might be right and I don't know enough about this new technology but you have to accept that I'm the decision maker and you have to live with it.' I was frustrated with the decision, as I felt it was 'obvious' that we should upgrade. However, it taught me to accept the decision and move on; you spend a lot of time at work, and it's just not healthy to harbour a grudge when a decision doesn't go your way. At the same company, I learned much from the purchasing manager, who was a master of negotiation. One of his favourite challenges to any of my project spend was 'Why buy a Rolls-Royce when a Mondeo will do the job?' Having had such a positive experience of mentoring throughout my career, I've always tried to 'pay it forward' and encourage others who are just starting out in their career. This book forms part of that ethos.

Deeper reasons

There's one more significant reason why we put together a plan to retire early and have the chance to enjoy life a little more before old age kicked in. On my 17th birthday, I visited my dad in hospital after he had undergone the first of two heart bypasses. Similarly, my father-in-law had a stroke at 52, which left him disabled in his movement and speech. Both were workaholics and weren't able to enjoy a traditional retirement. On many occasions in my later years at Amazon, when I was working late into the night (as many did, and still do) I'd say to Lou 'I'll just be another 30 minutes', and she would retort 'I'll write that on your gravestone – "I gave my final half hour to Jeff Bezos!"'

There's also a sense of morality and ownership, even though some might think of it as more political. In my mind it's not; it's about how you contribute to society. At heart, I'd be called a capitalist over a socialist, on the basis that I believe you need wealth creators to build businesses, pay tax and grow an economy that has sufficient funding to support the less well off. I also believe we're free to choose what we spend our money on; however, that includes ownership of how we fund our lifestyles. For that reason, I choose to pay for private dental cover and chose to pay additional contributions into my pension. In the same way that my parents supported me through school and university, ultimately it gave me good career choices and I've contributed back through my taxes.

We had a lodger a few years back who was a genuinely nice guy but quite vocal in his opinions and on one occasion (while watching the evening news) we discussed pension contributions and he said it had nothing to do with him: 'Once I've paid the bills and put food on the table, what's left is for me to spend on myself.' I asked him how he might fund his retirement and he said (again), 'Not my problem; it's the state's responsibility to look after me in my old age.'

We all have different views and I try not to be too judgemental when they differ from mine, particularly when related to finances, but I feel strongly that personal ownership is important, not just with money but also in relation to your role in society. Being judgemental goes both ways, though, and I feel equally frustrated when people say 'It's OK for you, you're rich', as though it's just fallen into our lap. Although I'll admit I've been guilty of this too. At university, the parents of a housemate went on a round-the-world cruise for their 25th wedding anniversary. His dad ran a successful family business so my girlfriend and I both commented that it was easy for them 'because they were rich'. My mate explained that his dad had started a 25-year savings plan after his wedding in order to fund it. I recall it was £20 a month, which was a reasonable amount at the time and showed long-term commitment plus a shrewd financial mind. That same university housemate has just been on a similar holiday for his own 25th anniversary and I smiled inwardly when friends said it's all right for them 'because they're rich'. Yes, they could afford this extravagant holiday but the fact is that their approach to money, the financial decisions they've made and the prioritisation of their spending has resulted in their wealth.

We all make choices every day – some short term, others longer term. Through this book I'm aiming to give you the tools to make some more informed choices for a stronger financial future, whatever your beliefs. I hope this has given you a flavour of my background and a few of the things that have influenced my thinking. I'd like to do some good with this book and if I can help a handful of people think again about their finances, make a few changes and have a more secure, confident future, then that will do for me.

Key takeaways

- → Take ownership of your plan – don't rely on others to do it for you.
- → Learn from others – even small things can make a difference if they resonate with you.
- → The plan is long term and the 'big picture' goal is a more confident financial future.

Where do I start?

Chapter 2

The basics

In Charles Dickens' book *David Copperfield,* first published in 1850, Mr Micawber states:

> 'Annual income twenty pounds, annual expenditure nineteen [pounds] nineteen [shillings] and six [pence], result happiness. Annual income twenty pounds, annual expenditure twenty pounds [n]ought and six, result misery.'

This concept is simple. As I've hinted at, this book isn't just about better financial management; it's also about your overall health and wellbeing and society in general. The Dickens example is analogous to dieting, which you could argue simply means to eat less and exercise more (or consume fewer calories). To quote a more recent fictional character, Jennifer Saunders' Edina Monsoon in *Absolutely Fabulous,* 'Well, if it was that simple, sweetie, everyone would be doing it.' But if you don't stick to the basics and have a sneaky chocolate biscuit here, a new pair of shoes there, before long you're slightly overweight, out of breath... or, in money terms, starting to feel stressed about your finances getting out of control.

So how do you go about fixing this mindset? The challenge is twofold. First, there's a lot of conflicting advice out there; and second, this stuff isn't really taught in schools and no one (at least in the UK) receives any structured education about money management. This second point is exacerbated by fears of litigation after giving the wrong advice. If you talk to any finance professional, they'll often cage your options with so many safety nets you might feel as if you'd be better off sticking your money under the mattress! I'm being slightly tongue in cheek here, as there are good advisors out there, including many independent ones, but the fact is that investments go up and down and no one can predict the future, nor which investment will do better than another. It's broadly similar to dieting (again) – if there was a single diet book that worked for everyone, there would be no need for any new diet books, yet they keep on coming.

Investment managers (finance professionals whom you can pay for advice) often talk about asset classes or sectors of investment. Consider the table opposite, showing the best and worst performing sectors (and their respective returns) for the ten years to 2019, plus the performance of global equities (shares) over the same period for comparison. There's very little consistency but it's common to see a class performing well one year after a poor year and vice versa. Although even this is a fairly loose trend, as demonstrated by the UK Smaller Companies class. If you were asked to pick one sector to invest in over the next 12 months, which would you choose? Or which sector would you pick to give you the most consistent returns over the next five years? Difficult, isn't it?

It's important to note that investments have variable performance and whatever anyone says to you, it's impossible to guarantee returns. Investment managers aim to do just this – analyse the market and predict which sector will perform better – but their performance is equally variable and you normally pay a premium for them to try. Note that there's no penalty for (their) failure either, as they're covered by the phrase 'investments may go down as well as up', so you're funding their decisions. You might win big or lose a little but they get paid anyway! There's an argument that you might be able to shorten the odds of better performance a little but that's as far as it goes. Looking at global equity performance (a broad selection of large global companies), although there have been two years of losses, some years have shown impressive returns. Over this ten-year horizon, this asset class has returned an average of 10.4%. This long-term positive performance is a theme I will revisit in a later chapter.

Year	Best performing asset class	%	Worst performing asset class	%	Global Equity Performance
2010	UK Smaller Companies	30.8%	UK Gilts	5.9%	15.5%
2011	UK Index-linked Gilts	21.8%	Emerging Markets	-19.1%	-9.4%
2012	UK Smaller Companies	22.6%	UK Index-linked Gilts	0.3%	9.8%
2013	UK Smaller Companies	37.3%	UK Gilts	-5 3%	21.8%
2014	UK Index-linked Gilts	18.7%	UK Smaller Companies	-1.6%	7.4%
2015	Japan	15.8%	Emerging Markets	-9.8%	4.0%
2016	Emerging Markets	33.1%	UK Smaller Companies	8.5%	24.0%
2017	UK Smaller Companies	26.7%	Global Bonds	1.6%	14 2%
2018	UK Gilts	-0.1%	Europe	-12.4%	-5.8%
2019	UK Smaller Companies	26.2%	Global Bonds & UK Index-Linked Gilts	5.9%	22.3%

Figure 1: Best and worst performing investment sectors over ten years (source: Hargreaves Lansdown)

I'm not here to tell you what to do with your money but I am going to help you analyse your way of life, your needs and wants, and then build a plan to fund a lifestyle that's tailored to you. I'll also give you the mechanisms to make more informed financial decisions, track your progress and give you a greater degree of money confidence that can lead to a happier and less stressful life.

In terms of what to invest in, you have two choices: make the decision yourself or ask a financial advisor. Financial advisors can be independent or tied to a specific range of funds and investments, and all vary in the way they charge. Unfortunately there's little in the way of free advice. Although I have managed my own finances for a long time, I'm not against getting professional advice and have done so several times. However, my two golden rules would be to:

1. use a recognised independent financial advisor who is regulated by the Financial Conduct Authority
2. really understand what it is you're asking for and challenge the answer.

This second point is important as there's no blanket advice; it should all be tailored to the financial outcome you want to achieve. It's analogous to asking a personal trainer to devise a plan for you; it will be different whether you want to increase your stamina, build muscle or train for a marathon. Similarly, there will be different advice for pensions or reducing your inheritance tax liability. Equally, when I say 'Challenge the answer', I want you to be bold enough to ask 'But what does that really mean for me in cold, hard cash?' There have been many times when I've not understood the jargon of a financial answer and I always ask for clarification in simple English. 'What could this realistically be worth in x years, or what is the genuine risk of me losing money?'

So this is how it all started for me. Back in the mid-1990s, when I was IT manager at the wheel manufacturer, we had a raft of apprentices who would be rotated around the different departments to gain experience. I'd normally start the first conversation with something like 'Hi, tell me what you'd like to do with your life – what are you interested in doing?' The response, typical of a 16- or 17-year-old was 'Dunno', and the cockier ones often threw it back at me, asking 'What do you want to do with *your* life?' So I told them I wanted a career that allowed me to drive a nice car that I could afford to replace every five or six years (at this point, I was just starting out and had a 12-year-old Vauxhall Nova), a biggish house so I could have people round (I was renting a two-up, two-down terrace at the time) and a garden in which I could relax. I also wanted to eat out at a nice restaurant with friends every few weeks, have one or two foreign holidays a year and be able to afford nice presents for friends and family. Oh, and I also wanted to get married. Every single one of the apprentices replied 'I want the same thing.' My response was 'Great, now you have a plan; you just have to figure out what that lifestyle will cost and how you're going to earn the money to fund it.' So this is how you do it.

Step 1: Work out what you want (and what your partner wants)

The key point here is that everyone is different, so there's no simple template. You may hate gardening and want a city centre flat close to pubs and clubs. You might want a large family and a house in the country. You might have no interest in cars and be happy with a ten-year-old diesel Golf or, alternatively, hanker after an Aston Martin. Your idea of relaxing might be reading, running or playing football. For a holiday, it could be skiing in Switzerland, lying on a beach in the Mediterranean or fell walking in the Brecon Beacons. The list is endless.

Of course, your 17-year-old self is going to have fairly

optimistic aspirations but as you get older, into your twenties and thirties, you'll begin to hone these plans into a more solid idea of what you want out of life. It doesn't matter if this changes over time; it probably will, but the fundamental theme will likely remain the same. It's what makes you happy and ultimately what you'd ideally like to spend your non-working time doing.

There's also a big fork in the road that you'll hit at least once and likely several times: when you're in a relationship. I'll cover this in more detail in Chapter 7 but suffice it to say it's fundamental that you have a conversation with your partner about what they want out of life. I'm not saying don't have fun while you're young, free and single – but when you get to the point where you're in a serious relationship, you really need to make sure you're both on similar pages. You don't have to have exactly the same ideas but they should broadly align, otherwise you're pretty much guaranteed to start falling out further down the road. Two of the common reasons for relationship breakdowns are a lack of communication and a difference in priorities. Most big financial decisions or goals are long term; therefore they need to be prioritised and agreed upon – so talk about them.

Later on, when you reach your forties or fifties, you'll hopefully be approaching paying off your mortgage, your kids may be out of your hair and you'll start thinking about retirement. It's still the same concept but the plan flips from one where you've been acquiring assets (paying the mortgage, earning a salary, investing in your pension) and you start consuming (spending). This is the 'twilight' phase of your plan and there's a lot of varied data available on typical spending levels in this phase; an example is shown in Figure 2. For either a single person or a couple it suggests the annual cost of living for three different levels of lifestyle, together with a London weighting.

Budget cost of living (2022)	Single Person	Couple
MINIMUM: Covers all your needs, with some left over for fun	**£12,800** LONDON £14,300	**£19,900** LONDON £22,400
MODERATE: More financial security and flexibility	**£23,300** LONDON £28,300	**£34,000** LONDON £41,400
COMFORTABLE: More financial freedom and some luxuries	**£37,300** LONDON £40,900	**£54,500** LONDON £56,500

Figure 2: Budgeting your cost of living in retirement (Pensions and Lifetime Savings Association 2023)

These are quite generic numbers and won't be applicable to everyone, but it's a good guideline to start from. Approximately five years ago, Lou and I did a deep financial review and some lifestyle profiling with a big-name investment company and the feedback was that whichever way you cut it, holidays, socialising, cars or whatever, most couples come out at an estimated £36,000 per year of expenditure, so I believe you can take this as a fair benchmark.

It's helpful to pause for breath here and acknowledge that this isn't all about money. Yes, it's a fundamental part of it but while it's commonly said that 'money can't buy you happiness', it certainly unlocks many more options and choices. For this reason, it forms a large part of my approach to life and not just to increase the balance in our bank account. I came across a better quote the other day: 'Being rich is having money, but being wealthy is having time.' Later in the book I'll discuss value, which is generally about the value of the brands or products we buy but it's also about valuing your time. At this stage, I'd ask you to commit to spending the time to look through your finances and work on making a plan as it will pay you dividends (no pun intended) later down the line. We all have the same 24 hours in the day but you have a large say in how you spend that time, so make it count.

Step 2: Set some targets

These don't necessarily have to be direct numerical ones; they might, for example, be paying off the mortgage or clearing a credit card debt. Again, a target can and will change over time but at least you have something to track to. If you know what you're aiming for, you can monitor progress and you'll know when you've achieved it. Having a meaningful target is better than a more vague goal such as 'I want to manage my money better'.

I was recently chatting to a good friend (a farmer turned accountant) who has also retired early about whether this approach was anything new, and he summed it up in a very Micawber-ish way: 'Spend less than you earn and invest the rest wisely.' So to achieve the core elements of your financial goals, you'll need to:

- spend less
- earn more
- understand investments.

I'll deal with these in more detail in later chapters – but how to start? You'll need to know (roughly) where you want to be and then understand the three core mechanisms (or levers) that affect how to get there. So how do you start? Primarily, you need to work out your baseline or financial starting point.

Step 3: Know your financial position

This is where you have to sit down with a pen and paper or a spreadsheet and document everything you know in relation to your finances. Some are straightforward: bank account, mortgage balance, credit cards and so on, but you need to capture everything – car loans, pensions, premium bonds, ISAs, savings accounts, etc. Plus, you need to document any big assets that you own or are on your way to owning. Primarily this will be your flat or house (which you're paying towards with your mortgage, unless you're renting, in which case ignore the property figure). It could also include your car but only if you own it outright or have a loan that's paying towards it and you'll own the car at the end of the loan. If it's leased or on a similar personal contract purchase (PCP) agreement, don't include the value of the car because you won't own it at the end of the contract.

You should arrange this in two columns (see Figure 3): what you own that's of value and what you owe to others. Column 1 minus column 2 is your net worth. Don't be tempted to ignore or hide anything and don't worry too much at this stage about the net worth figure; think of it as the starting point, not your end state.

What you own of value		What you owe	
House	250,000	Mortgage balance	175,000
Car	12,000	Car loan	7,500
Bank account	-1,500	Credit card #1	6,000
Pension* (company)	65,000	Credit card #2	500
ISA	1,000		
Premium Bonds	500		
Total	327,000	Total	189,000
Net worth			£138,000

* The assumption here is that this is a defined contribution pension – see Chapter 6 for the definition and the differences in pension types.

Figure 3: Figuring out your net worth

This exercise might be an eye opener in itself and possibly a little scary, particularly if you've been avoiding facing up to the reality of some debts or loans. If you're in a relationship, this is also the point at which you need to decide whether to do this as a couple or as individuals.

Just be mindful of what's in joint names and work out the figures accordingly. An important point to note here is to remember where you got the data from, as this is something you should be doing at regular intervals so that you can keep track of your progress. Technology has massively helped here, so take the time to register for online banking access so that you can easily get an updated balance with a few clicks. It will be more accurate than relying on an annual paper statement and will help you see changes more quickly. I believe (and suggest) you should track this every month (quarterly at a minimum), which is not too onerous once you get into the habit – but it's up to you. Put a date in the diary (first Saturday of every month?) and set some time aside to do it.

This aligns with my appreciation of Japanese production methods, in particular the process of continual improvement, or what's become known as Deming's wheel (aka the PDCA cycle): Plan, Do, Check, Act. In our situation, or in financial terms, the approach could be defined as:

- **Plan:** know your overall goal, understand your spending and earnings.
- **Do**: implement changes to your spending and earnings.
- **Check:** track your progress against your overall goal every month, or at least quarterly.
- **Act:** make changes to your actions if your original actions are not reflected in your results towards your goals.

Step 4: Know what you spend (and what you earn)

Much like working out your base financial position, you also need a good picture of what you spend in a given period. Again, this is likely to be another eye opener so you need to be honest with yourself (or yourselves) and not hide anything. As above, be sure you're consistent about whether you're doing this as individuals or as a couple. Historically, this would mean wading through a year's worth of bank or credit card statements, not to mention chequebook stubs, but it's much easier now to get downloads and either print them or put them into a spreadsheet.

You need to do this at least once a year, as some expenditure is annual (eg Christmas, birthdays or servicing the car) whereas other spending is more consistent throughout the year. If possible, it would be better to analyse two years (or even three – but you won't get much additional insight beyond this). Don't be tempted to ignore exceptional items unless you know they really are one-offs and unlikely to recur in the next five years or so. Once you have your data, convert it into a monthly figure.

You can tailor the list to suit (for example, you might have child maintenance payments or school fees) but I suggest using the list below as a starting point. Note that the last category is 'unknown spending' – this is typically cash you withdraw and have no idea where it actually goes. I'm not particularly against using cash but I much prefer using a card so that I can track my spending.

- mortgage or rent
- insurance (life, house, car)
- bank or credit card fees/interest
- council tax

- utilities (water/oil/gas/electricity)
- household/garden maintenance (including buying new appliances)
- food (home groceries from supermarkets, including household consumables)
- food and drink (eating out at restaurants/pubs)
- phone/broadband/mobile
- TV licence and subscriptions
- other subscriptions (gym, magazines)
- clothing, healthcare and beauty
- holidays and days out
- car and transport costs (loan payments, petrol, servicing, train fares)
- gifts and presents
- unknown spending

Similarly, you need to do the same with income and in most cases this is much simpler, particularly if you're in full-time or regular employment. If you're contracting or have variable income (for example, through overtime or commissions-based sales, or are self-employed) take an honest view over a reasonable period of time. Typically, categories might look like this:

- income from main employment
- savings interest (or cashback)
- benefits (eg child benefit, child tax credits)
- other income (such as part-time work, second jobs or 'side hustles')
- gifts

There are several budget tools and templates available online to help you with this, although the categories above should be sufficient for now. Don't worry about setting a 'budget' at this point; what's important is to know what you spend now before you can tackle how and where you can reduce your spending.

Spend less, earn more, invest wisely

Over the next few chapters, I'll tackle the three core elements of spending less, earning more and investing wisely. The fundamental part of spending less (after knowing what you spend) is realising what you're overspending on. There are the essentials: food, a roof over your head, electricity, etc. But we live in a highly commercialised society and the pressure to make additional or discretionary spending is ever present. This spending isn't really necessary and there are many tricks (or marketing strategies) that companies use to encourage us to spend more. What's more, whatever 'it' is, they also manage to convince you that you do actually need it, it's great value and you should congratulate yourself for buying it! Needless to say, I disagree with a lot of this and will walk you through some of these marketing concepts to help you rethink what you spend your money on, with the ultimate goal of helping you to spend less.

The flip side of the coin is how to earn more. I'll explore how to build a career plan, or at least to manage your career path with the objective of earning a better base salary, with methods of achieving regular, incremental increases. Unfortunately, the last time most of us were given any career advice was at school but this wasn't really the best time for it, not least because we probably didn't really know what we wanted to do and were more interested in getting our first girlfriend or boyfriend or passing our driving test. Think of the 'Earning more' chapter as revisiting your careers advisor but at a time when you're more likely to understand the impact of your choices and decisions and you're in more of a position to act on them. And don't worry if you don't have A-levels or a degree – experience, attitude and approach will advance your career more than qualifications on a piece of paper.

Having started to explain how to better manage your money and increase your confidence in making sound financial decisions, it's worth pausing to talk a little about motivation. I'm not a motivational coach, but I can share with you learnings from my own experience – however, you'll have to figure a bit of this out for yourself. You need to think about what motivates you because if you're going to follow a long-term plan, it's more likely to succeed if you tailor your approach to match what motivates you. This isn't exactly scientific but it's about knowing what holds your interest; it might be as simple as a straightforward goal such as paying off your mortgage by the time you're 50, or clearing your credit card debt by the end of the year. Or it could be a little broader, such as trying not to buy any new clothes for the next year, using your car less and walking more often, or throwing away less food. Think about it and talk to your family or partner about it, as it's not only enlightening but can also help elsewhere in your life. For example (and unsurprisingly), I hate wasting money or spending when I don't really need to, and it's a key motivator for me in any decision.

When I was little, I was involved in a car crash with my mum. This was long before the days of compulsory seatbelts and I was thrown forward and hit the dashboard, breaking my front teeth, which had only just come through. About 15 years later, I was in a fight at school and broke a front tooth after my head was smashed into a desk. Unfortunately, as this was already my second set of front teeth it meant having to have them capped. Everything was fine, with the cap holding firm through my teens, early adulthood and through to midlife. About five years ago, I tripped over in B&Q and landed on my face, breaking a tooth again. Over the next few years, I had to have it refitted several times, each time bonding the new tooth on less and less of the old one and each time the dentist assured me it would 'last for years.' Since I now pay for my dentistry, I'm paranoid that it will fail again and I'll get another large bill to fix it. This has resulted in me finally stopping chewing my nails or 'cutting' Sellotape off the roll with my teeth. Trying to avoid another unnecessary dental bill has definitely changed my behaviour.

One bit of homework for you to do is to work out what motivates you so that you can build this into your plan. I'll come back to this in the section about managing and tracking your progress, in order to find and use metrics that resonate with you so that you're more engaged and have a better chance of success. The last thing I want to do is tell you how you should do it and for you to then lose interest because it's not aligned with what makes you tick.

On FIRE

At this stage, some of you might be thinking that all of this sounds similar to a fairly well-known movement called Financial Independence and Retire Early, or FIRE as it's commonly called. The exact origins of the term are unclear, although many attribute it to the concepts outlined in the 1992 book *Your Money or Your Life* by Vicki Robin and Joe Dominguez. I'd argue that my approach is slightly different; it's a mindset change to your way of life, how you approach financial decisions, understanding true value for money, maximising your earning potential and understanding the budget you need to live a life that's fulfilling for you. Moreover, I don't want to just focus on the final outcome. I'm more interested in mechanisms that get you there, the confidence you have in understanding and making good financial decisions and therefore having more control over your financial future, whatever that may be.

But let's look at some definitions and you can make up your own mind. To many, FIRE in its pure form is about 'ultra saving' (maybe up to 70% of your income), living frugally and investing your savings with a view to stopping work as soon as possible, in some cases in your forties. In theory and practice, many people have done this and good luck to them. I'm conscious that we're only on this planet once and therefore, while not being too extravagant, I believe we should always schedule some time (and funds) to enjoy ourselves. A pure FIRE evangelist might want to live on bread and water and not take any holidays but it's a little too drastic for me and maybe for you too.

As ever, there are also variations on pure FIRE. There's FatFIRE and LeanFIRE. FatFIRE is when you retire early and live a lavish lifestyle ever after. LeanFIRE means to retire early but with an amount that allows you to lead a lean and simple lifestyle. FatFIRE does follow some similar principles to my approach but doesn't help you understand how finances work; instead, it focuses on some key numbers and rules. To 'achieve FatFIRE', received wisdom says you need to have 25 times your yearly spending in your investment portfolio. So if you wanted a 'retirement' or lifestyle of £36,000 a year, you'd need £900,000 in your pension/ISA/savings pot. This is a similar figure to the £1 million suggested to me many years ago, so perhaps it wasn't that far off the mark. The assumption of FatFIRE is that you'll enjoy a 'lavish lifestyle' once you've stopped working, whereas LeanFIRE is a more frugal version whereby you continue with a less extravagant but still comfortable lifestyle. The real difference is how quickly you can get there and since you need a larger pot of money for FatFIRE, it's easier to achieve LeanFIRE more quickly. But in my view, it sounds like a rather dull existence. It might be right for some, and arguably reducing consumption is a good thing for the planet, but I'm still in the camp of enjoying yourself once in a while.

As you can imagine, I'm on many online forums and groups that actively discuss FIRE, but for me it's far too technical. For example, these forums often discuss withdrawal strategies, relative investment returns from one type of fund structure over another, gilt yields in the long term and many more deeply financial topics.

This is a genuine example I came across on one UK site:

Question: If you fund your retirement from share investments (pensions and ISA), do you set up a regular sell order irrespective of what the share market is doing? If you also have three years of spending saved up in cash, do you stop your sell order when the market drops and don't resume until your cash buffer drops to a predetermined level or when the market recovers?

One of the responses: Deciding on the split between using up your cash buffer and liquidating investments is tricky. My modelling suggests that you should use up most of your cash immediately, leaving the investments in the market but keep a smaller buffer (three to six months?) for emergencies. I tried modelling various splits between assets and cash, including adjusting the split based on market values but couldn't improve upon using up the cash buffer initially. The spreadsheets for this were admittedly a bit messy. If you do the opposite and ignore the cash buffer to liquidate assets from the outset, the portion of your portfolio in cash immediately starts losing money in real terms and (except in a few very specific historical cases, from memory) the overall portfolio value never recovers compared to using the cash and leaving the assets to grow. It does depend on your withdrawal rate to some extent – if this is higher, then you're more exposed to a recession as you're taking out more assets while they're lower in value. But in nearly all cases, recessions did not last long enough to make it better to hang on to any cash above the emergency fund.

It is a valid question and I don't doubt the answer is a sensible one, but I lost the will to live halfway through the post. It's way too complicated for me and as I've said before, I'm no maths wizard. I'd much rather have a more simple approach to finance and not spend too much time with my head buried in a spreadsheet.

So that's a rapid overview of FIRE. While I've done the 'retire early' bit, I don't believe the ethos of my approach is the same; I prefer to think of it as having a better mindset about money rather than just focusing on an end goal. I'm also not convinced that you can step-change your lifestyle from ultra saving to extravagant spending without it all going horribly wrong. Imagine you don't go out to restaurants, don't eat takeaways, don't have holidays, rarely socialise, buy your clothes from a charity shop, go to bed at 8.00 pm to save energy and make a bar of soap last two months. In parallel, you're throwing every spare penny into your pension, ISA or other investments. You're now 48, you've got your calculator out and find you've hit the magic 25x multiple so you hand in your notice. What now? Go out and buy a Lamborghini, kit yourself out in designer clothes, get on first name terms with the maître d' of your local Michelin-starred restaurant and book a world cruise? You might do some or all of these but the challenge is that your spending will be uncontrolled as your new lifestyle is alien to you. It's like someone winning millions on the lottery and a few years later you read they've blown it all in a few short years on a lavish lifestyle that they're just not used to.

Sense-checking that last thought, I'll admit I'm not claiming to be perfect either; having worked on our plan for 20 years and more seriously for the past 10, it's difficult to stop saving (although you're somewhat limited, for example, in what you can save into your pension if you're no longer working) and start spending. However, we're learning and definitely enjoying trying! But we still use the same principles of understanding value in what we'll spend our money on – I go back to the example of buying our BMW; we could have bought a brand new 2.0 litre convertible and spent twice as much as we did but we didn't. We bought second hand and still intend to keep the car for five to ten years. We're having no less fun and we still do the same monthly review as we've always done, so we're comfortable we're not overshooting ourselves. So those are the basics of how to get a grip on your finances; now let's move on to putting it into practice.

Key takeaways

→ Work out your 'ideal lifestyle' (and what your partner wants too). This is your end goal but think about smaller, interim targets along the way.

→ Understand your financial position, your income and outgoings.

→ By all means seek financial advice but be clear on what you're asking for and how much it will cost. As a preference, use an independent financial advisor (see Resources).

Chapter 3

How to spend less

Now that you've reviewed your spending, you should have a broad idea of where your money is going, so you can start to look at ways of reducing it if you need to. Again, since everyone is different, so are your spending profiles, but there are some themes you can apply to most categories and start getting your spending under control. And to reiterate, this is only one side of the coin; to be financially better off, you can either spend less or earn more – and ideally both. Some of you may already be practising some of the approaches outlined below, so don't beat yourself up if you can't come up with a plan to trim thousands off your spending. Remember, this is about understanding what you spend your money on and controlling it better, not just as a one-time cut but changing the way you spend forever.

I'll cover the basic concepts here and add more detail about marketing and assessing value in the next chapter – but this is your starting point. This chapter is broken down into three sections: I'll start with some key themes and then tackle regular and discretionary spending. If you google 'money-saving tips' you'll find plenty of ideas, which are great but a little overwhelming and not relevant to everyone. They may also go into micro-saving such as cutting off the end of the toothpaste tube to eke out every last bit. Rather than include a huge list, I'll focus on bigger areas of spending that will drive the biggest impact or a behavioural change.

I like to view savings as an annual impact to help determine if it's worth my effort and I have a figure of £100 as a guide. If it's going to save me more than £100 over the year, then it's worthwhile doing it. If it's much less than this, I'm less inclined and likely to focus on something else.

There are several useful mantras about spending, with a couple of popular ones from Martin Lewis (from MoneySavingExpert), such as: 'Do I need it? Can I afford it? Will I use it? Is it worth it?' These are great but don't help you get under the skin of how to answer them and that's key to being able to change your spending habits. I prefer a much older quote from the 19th-century textile designer, writer and artist, William Morris: 'Have nothing in your houses that you do not know to be useful or believe to be beautiful.' This focuses on function but gives you a little latitude to have some things purely for pleasure.

Key themes

In addition to deciding what to buy, there's also how you buy. I don't know where it originated but I learned this expression from my father-in-law and it's often referred to as the 'iron triangle': 'You can have it fast, have it good, or have it cheap: pick two.' This reflects that whatever two you want (for example, speed and quality), you're going to have to compromise on the third (cost).

Thinking about general household goods (which take up a large portion of your necessary spend), typically you'll be shopping at supermarkets and convenience stores (or corner shops), with the supermarket being larger and offering lower prices due to economies of scale. Obviously, you're paying for the convenience of the more local corner shop and you're not incurring time and money travelling to an out of town supermarket, but you will pay higher prices and have less choice. How much higher varies dramatically but as a rule of thumb, think in terms of a 10% premium, with some things as much as 25% more expensive. These convenience stores have their place but if it's where you find yourself doing your regular shopping, I'd suggest rethinking where you shop.

Technology (and Covid-19) has created a third dimension in the form of the delivery app. A widely reported study by consumer watchdog *Which?* (2023) found that a basket of groceries was 38% more expensive when delivered by a rapid delivery service than the same items bought from the same store in person. Prices for a basket of ASDA groceries were 9% higher (Deliveroo and Just Eat) than the in-store price of £45.60, while Uber Eats were 19% more expensive at £54.39. This is a rapidly evolving marketplace and I predict more changes to come before they mature and find their place in our lifestyles – but be aware they're currently a hugely expensive habit to get into. If you find out where your local corner shop is, you might find it's not only cheaper but also quicker to walk or cycle there! In a similar vein, while the likes of Amazon have introduced the expectation of 'free delivery', never forget it's anything but free. The cost of getting an order to you (from any online retailer) is factored into the price you pay and, in Amazon's case, you're paying for a Prime subscription to fund this (noted, this covers more than just shipping but the point remains, it's not truly 'free').

Don't buy into brands

It's time for some more self-reflection and, as a precursor to the later chapter on marketing, don't discount the influence of peer pressure and buying into brands. In numerous cases, in taste testing (or where the brand is hidden), it's never a foregone conclusion that the most expensive or branded item is the most preferred. I'll admit I'll always have Heinz tomato ketchup with my fish and chips, so it's OK to allow yourself a small indiscretion every so often. And if you chased around looking for the 'best buy' for every different product, you'd spend your life in supermarkets and be constantly stressed trying to remember whether it was Aldi or Lidl that had had the best salad cream, so cut yourself a little slack. The gist of my argument is that branded goods are not always the best. I'm also up for a little subterfuge; if you have kids, buy your local supermarket ketchup and decant it into a Heinz bottle when they're in bed. You never know, it might just work! Try it with adults too; we have some friends who regularly shop at Waitrose ('because it's better'), so whenever they come round for dinner, we always buy everything from Lidl and have never had any complaints.

Knowing when to buy cheap and when to buy quality (and knowing the difference) is a subtle art and there are no hard and fast rules. But if you analyse your spending and give more thought to what you're buying, you'll subconsciously start to recognise what works for you. It's summed up brilliantly by Terry Pratchett in *Men at Arms: The Play* (1997), in which he argues that the rich remain rich because they spend less money, which sounds obvious but he explains it differently than you might expect. Buying a well-made pair of boots for £100 that would last more than 20 years is cheaper than buying an inferior pair for £25 that only lasts two years before you need to buy another pair. The point is, you have to have £100 to spend in the first place; in other words, you needed to be rich. If you can only afford £25 for an inferior pair, you could well end up spending £250 for boots over the course of 20 years. He called this the 'boots theory of socioeconomic unfairness.'

The first trick is not always assuming a well-known

brand equals quality. It's sometimes genuinely better quality (such as being made from higher specification raw materials) but not necessarily, with components often being exactly the same as a less premium brand. The second trick is to recognise frequency – how often are you going to use something? Longevity is disappearing in this ever more rapid world of fast fashion and technological advances but buying something once and keeping it for a long time is not only good for your wallet, it's better for the environment too.

Check your credit rating

Before we hit some big-spending topics, a quick comment on your credit rating: it can have a huge impact on your ability to secure better finance. In short, know what your credit score is, know how to influence it and check it regularly. Again, thanks to the internet, this has become easier to do and there are several free options, notably Clearscore and Experian. They all work on the same principles and I don't believe one is any better than the other. The mere fact that you're checking your score is key. The average UK score is currently around 585/1,000, so while it's obviously nice to know if you're 'above average' it's more important to actively manage your score, either improving it if it's a little low or maintaining it if it's good. Many factors impact your score, such as whether you miss a credit card payment, dip into any overdrafts, have county court judgements against you, opened a new account or bought something on finance that's triggered a credit search. I was actually a little surprised when ours came out at a perfect 1,000 earlier in the year, but even then it still dipped to below 900 for a few months as we'd paid for some holidays and a new bike, which maxed out our credit card. Despite our strong financial position, it was still deemed to be a 'red flag'. Take time to register and look through all the data. Most companies will go back and generate a historical profile, so you quickly get a good picture of your score profile and you have the ability to request corrections that might be negatively impacting your score (such as a bad debt against a previous owner of your property).

What's in a percentage rate?

Many of your larger purchases are likely to be financed at one time or another and the headline figure is normally the percentage rate. As ever, there are a variety of ways this can be expressed, most commonly an annual percentage rate or APR. There's also a variant used with mortgages, the annual percentage rate of charge or ARPC. It follows that an APR of 2% is better than 4% for a loan if all other conditions are equal, such as admin fees. A further variation is the annual equivalent rate or AER (sometimes also called the annual percentage yield or APY, as it's more commonly quoted in relation to savings and investments rather than loans).

Low percentage rates can be very seductive; however, they're a little tricky to unpick, particularly when the rate changes over a period of time – typically if an introductory rate is quoted. It's normally the headline-grabbing number of any finance deal but the length of term also plays a significant part and, for this reason, my preferred approach to any finance deal is to ask the simple question 'How much am I paying in total over the full term?' For example, a loan or purchase of £5,000 in value at 7.3% APR over 36 months would give you a monthly payment of £154.54 and a total repayment figure of £5,563.36. Or, in other words, it will cost you £536.36 to borrow the money. If you took the loan out over five years (same APR), the monthly repayments would be £99.16 (less per month) but the total repaid would increase by £386.43 to £5,949.79.

Therefore, there are two decision points to consider in any big purchase via finance. First, what are the monthly payments and can you afford them as part of your regular budget? And second, what's the total cost and does it represent value for money for what you're buying? Sometimes you just have to accept that in order to afford something, you end up paying a little more. This is fine, providing you know that you're making a conscious decision and that it's a worthwhile trade-off. I find it's a good way to evaluate if I really need or want something. Am I prepared to pay the 'financed' price for it?

Regular spending

Starting with the biggest first, let's cover some high-impact areas of core spending. To reiterate, I'm not going to tell you what's the cheapest or best deal; I want to help you understand how finance works in each category so that you're better informed and can make the right decision for you. There are many comparison sites out there but fundamentally they all focus on the cheapest deal and while I'm not saying cheap isn't good, I don't believe they help you understand what you're actually paying for.

Mortgages

Banks will lend you money but never forget that they want to make money out of you and are good at hiding how they do this. Interest rates are a key element of mortgages and we're coming out of a long period of historically low rates, so it was always going to be painful when they went up from such a low base. At the time of writing, the Bank of England base rate is 5%, which I consider low against the 8% we were paying when we had our largest mortgage balance and very low against my parents' mortgage rate of 15%, which I recall from my childhood.

Property has historically proved to be a good investment over the long term and, despite the scary rates, I still took my dad's advice and got onto the property ladder as soon as I was able to while in my first job. Over the past 15 years, average house prices have risen from around £155,000 in 2008 to £290,000 in 2023. For most people, it's going to be a struggle to get on the first rung of the ladder, let alone keeping up with changing payments, but you need to build affordability into your plan and approach mortgage payments as a priority. I couldn't get a mortgage when I was looking to buy my first house, as no one would lend against my combination of salary, deposit and the cost of the house. I was a little cheeky in that I asked to see the company's finance director, explained my position, stated that I liked working there and wanted to stay, and was there any chance of a small pay rise to allow me to get the mortgage? I remember him saying that no one had ever asked him that before but I must have made a good impression because he agreed!

One of the single most important decisions we made, which has given us our financial freedom, was to focus on paying off our mortgage. The interest you pay to the bank is huge and the sooner you can reduce it, the better. So it's time for some maths to show you what you're really paying for and why it should be your number one target.

Consider a house worth £250,000. You have a £25,000 (10%) deposit and a repayment mortgage over 25 years at 6%. A quick online calculator gives us a figure of £1,449.68 per month. This is where most people stop. But think about the numbers: 25 years, 12 months per year at £1,449.68 a month – that's £434,904 in total. You borrowed £225,000 (house value less the deposit) and you're paying the bank £209,904 in interest. Yes, they're lending you a large sum of money (and not without risk) but do you realise what you're really paying in total? It's nearly the same as the value of the house! If you managed to squeeze another £5,000 onto the deposit, you'd save £9,666 in interest payments. The effect of overpaying can't be underestimated either. In the example above, overpaying an additional £200 a month would allow you to pay off your mortgage nearly six years earlier, saving £56,000 in interest payments.

There's another hidden cost of the repayment mortgage, especially if you think you're saving money by remortgaging frequently. You're probably not. The average person in the street might reasonably assume that their mortgage balance would be reduced equally each year; in other words, they will have paid back 1/25th of the mortgage every year, or £9,000 a year in our example. I'm sorry to say they're wrong. Thanks to the cunning way that financial institutions construct their mortgages, they decide to split it differently through the term of the mortgage, with a heavy bias towards interest in the early years. Using the same example above, in the first year, you'll have paid £17,396 to the bank and whereas you might have thought (hoped) that £9,000 was going towards reducing what you owed on the house, the bank only paid £4,005 against the house and took the remaining £13,391 as interest. And it continues like this on a sliding scale towards the end of the mortgage. In fact, it's not until year 15 that you actually breach the £9,000 payment against the property. But who keeps the same mortgage for 15 years? Unless you're locked in for five or 10 years, many people remortgage every three or four years, often with a hefty admin fee and the lure of the interest rate they're paying. What they're missing is that they're effectively extending the life of their mortgage (and increasing the total interest paid) without realising it. Figure 4 demonstrates a typical repayment schedule, clearly showing that in the early years you're paying much more interest than reducing your loan size.

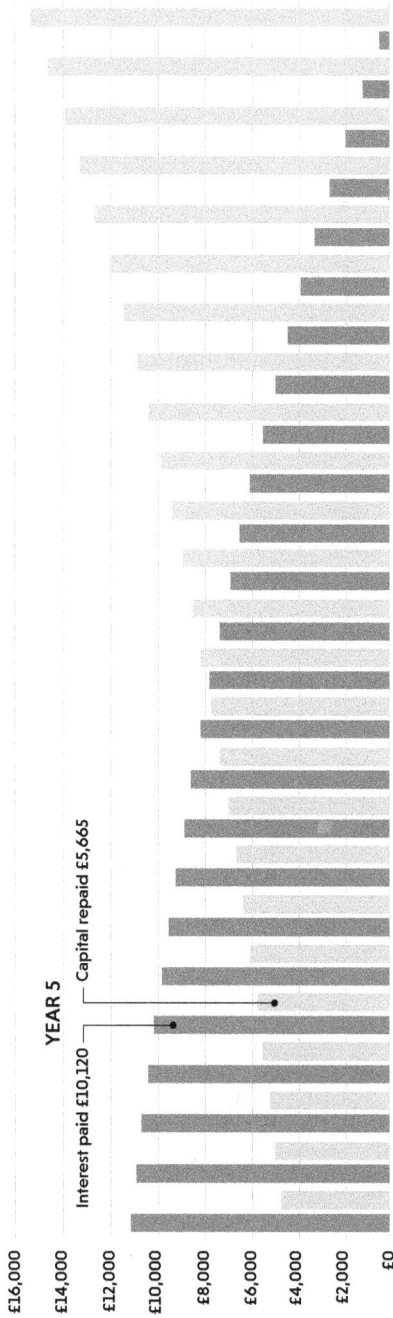

Figure 4: Mortgage interest and capital repayments over 25 years on a typical £225,000 repayment mortgage

So I'm in favour of overpaying your mortgage as much as you can (although most banks don't like this because it dents their profits, so they limit you to a maximum of 10% a year in overpayments) and not remortgaging too often. One critical point to note (and to avoid a sneaky banker 'trick') is to check with your mortgage company that any overpayments will be deducted from the amount owed and the interest element reduced accordingly. Some have been known to recalculate the mortgage balance annually and to hold the overpayments as prepayments against interest, generously allowing you a payment holiday in the future – in other words, they're taking your money without any benefit to you.

I prefer interest-only mortgages, with the caveat that you must have the discipline to make overpayments against the capital amount. With the same mortgage, it would cost you £1,125 in interest payments in month one but as soon as you make an overpayment, it comes off the amount owed and the interest payable reduces. An interest-only mortgage is even better if you can tie it to a bank account, where it becomes an offset mortgage. Here your current account balance offsets the mortgage balance (effectively reducing it), which maximises the effect of reducing your mortgage balance. If you have any, you can even use it to spice up your savings; rather than having savings earning 3% interest, why not hold that balance in your offset account and effectively earn 6%? The benefit is paying off your mortgage earlier and significantly reducing the amount of interest you pay. It also could save you some tax as you won't be getting 'paid' any interest on your savings, rather you pay less interest on your mortgage.

In summary, I can't pay your mortgage for you but I can open your eyes to the value of prioritising paying it off early. However, not everyone agrees with this approach. A quick internet search of financial strategies will corroborate this, but I'm in the camp of 'pay off your biggest debts as soon as possible' and I can guarantee you that paying off your mortgage is the biggest stress relief there is.

Car finance

Whether you're a petrolhead or view your car as purely a means to travel from A to B, UK consumers appear to have drifted into accepting car finance as a default option and changing vehicles more frequently. Data published in 2023 by the Finance and Leasing Association shows that, despite a falling number of deals, the total new business for car finance in 2022 ballooned to more than £40 billion. What's more worrying is that, unlike with mortgages, there doesn't appear to be the same level of due diligence and affordability checking to prevent people from sleepwalking into an expensive way of buying a car. Some might argue that it's a cheap way into car ownership, but in reality a lot of car finance isn't ownership, it's leasing (renting) and ties you into forever paying 'rent' for your car. Putting some statistics around this, new car drivers financed on average £25,325 in 2022, with more than 2.2 million drivers entering car finance agreements, up 3% on 2021. This happened while we were in the middle of a cost of living crisis. And what does everyone know about buying a brand new car? Yes, it loses a massive chunk of value and depreciates the moment you drive off the forecourt. Data changes quickly but an internet search shows some interesting trends: of the top ten slowest depreciating cars, all cost more than £50k and half of those cost north of £100k, so you have to dig deep not to lose money (retaining between 65–80% of their list price after three years). This chimes with the earlier example of buying boots; if you can afford a more expensive car, it retains its value better. At the other end of the scale, the bottom ten only retained 30–40% of their value after three years.

Car	Term	Miles	Deposit	Monthly	Total	+Maintenance	Total
Fiat 500	36m	8,000	£2,000	£326/m	£13,510	£364/m	£14,878
Audi A5	36m	8,000	£4,000	£679/m	£27,865	£703/m	£28,729
Audi A5	48m	5,000	£5,000	£571/m	£31,937	£608/m	£33,713

Figure 5: Car finance illustration

Let's take a 1.0 litre Fiat 500 as a budget example and a nice 2.0 litre Audi A5 Coupe as one you'd probably prefer. Looking at some sample lease deals via *Parkers* price guide (summarised in Figure 5), the baby Fiat comes in at £326 a month over three years or £13,510 in total costs, or £14,878 in total if you have inclusive maintenance. On the other hand, the Audi looks more of a stretch at £703 a month, so you ask the dealer if they can do you 'a better deal' and after a bit of number crunching (and highly likely having left you for a while 'to go and speak with the manager') they come back having shaved more than £100 off the deal and we're now looking at a more palatable £571 a month. Great deal, eh? And for the same car – what a bargain! Except you're now in a four-year deal, only allowed to do 5,000 miles a year, have increased your deposit by £1,000 and don't have maintenance included. And the (hidden) cost of this better deal? An additional £3,208 in the dealer's pocket, plus 14p per mile for every mile you do over 20,000 miles.

Against this, a typical three-year-old model with similar mileage would cost you approximately £8k for the Fiat and £23k for the Audi. If you look at the higher depreciating models, you could get a dependable three-year-old (36k miles) Fiat Tipo for under £8k (list £22k) or Peugeot 508 for just over £16k (list £40k) and keep it for five or six years. I know this is a fairly dull option but when you're stuck in traffic on the motorway, the only real difference is the badge on the steering wheel and a bit of the switchgear. When people say to me I've only retired 'because I'm rich', that's not true. I could afford to retire because I've driven my fair share of second-hand cars: Toyota Carina, Honda Civic, Renault Laguna, Vauxhall Vectra, Ford Mondeo and Vauxhall Insignia. I've never had a leased or PCP finance deal but in my early days I financed a pure car loan to purchase a car outright and kept it for five years or more. I used the money saved to overpay on our offset mortgage. Aside from what you buy and how you fund it, keeping your car for longer is also a considerable factor and one that isn't encouraged by the structure of many car finance products. One mechanism to reduce the monthly cost of a deal is to have a 'balloon payment' at the end of the term, which you can pay to own the car outright. Unfortunately, at the end of your deal, you might not think paying several thousand for a three-year-old car is such a great deal, particularly when the dealer suggests you could roll this over and be driving a nice new one instead. It's easy to understand how tempting this is! You may be lucky and find that your car is worth more than the balloon payment and therefore, if you still like the car, it's a good deal. However, my hunch is that many are lured into a larger balloon figure by virtue of lower monthly payments.

Aside from going to your local dealer, there are a couple of ways in which you could reduce the price of whatever car you decide to buy. I've used all three methods and saved around £20,000 in total against the market selling price. First is using an internet broker, who will buy the car direct from the manufacturer, skipping the dealer. You need to know what model you want and you can't test drive the car but there's nothing to stop you researching your choice at local garages to help you choose and then buying direct. This works particularly well for traditional (some might say dull) fleet vehicles. I bought my Vauxhall Insignia this way and saved £7,000 against the list price, where my local dealer only offered me a £2,000 discount. There are several brokers to choose from, with the discounts varying by model. You won't get much off a newly released premium brand but you could find a bargain among more mainstream models.

The second option is a little niche but you might be lucky. It's increasingly common for employers to offer 'partner benefits' alongside your pay package and this can range from gym membership and mobile phone contracts to new car deals. If you're looking and you get an offer that matches what you want, you can get a great deal. I was extremely lucky as I was looking for my BMW when such an email with offers came through – the timing was perfect. I followed it up with a quote and bought the car. The discount was exceptionally generous. Together with the current trend of increasing second-hand car values, after three years it's worth exactly what I paid for it – zero depreciation. I've been very fortunate with this deal, and while it won't work for everyone, you could be lucky.

Finally, to negate the depreciation most new cars suffer, buying second hand is an option, with auctions being a cheaper way to buy. However, there is some risk in this and not everyone is comfortable with this approach. There are some companies who will broker this for you, help you find a car that matches your requirements and then bid, prepare and deliver the car for you. We did this for the Z4; we bought it under the price limit we'd set, the broker serviced it, put on a fresh MOT and delivered it to us, saving several thousand compared to buying a similar model from a dealer.

I also have to address the topic of electric vehicles (EVs), as they're becoming increasingly popular, not least because of government legislation banning the sale of petrol and diesel-engined cars coming in the near future, but they're often quoted as being cheaper to run as well as being more environmentally friendly. I don't believe the technology is anywhere near mature enough, which is leading to some EVs depreciating heavily, although that could benefit you if you buy second hand. Due to the impact of battery manufacture, I'm also not totally convinced about their environmental credentials, nor is the charging infrastructure anywhere near ready to cope with all-electric traffic. However, if you do a lot of local urban mileage, have off-street parking, solar panels and a good charging tariff, I can see the attraction. We don't have one, although we do have e-bikes, and as a result we use our cars much less; overall, we think this amounts to a bigger environmental saving. Buying an EV is a personal choice but it's worth thinking about how you buy one.

As you may have gathered, I'm not a fan of the current car finance landscape, nor the current lifestyle marketing that promotes cars as a commodity you can change as often as your shoes. The choice is yours – do you want to spend a lot of your disposable income on impressing your mates or do you want to save a serious amount of money? There's also a slight contradiction in that we have bought both new and second hand, when used is the cheaper option. We've chosen to buy new a couple of times when we knew we were going to keep the car for more than ten years or rack up a big mileage; in those situations, we felt it made sense. Plus, of course, we never paid full dealer price.

Mobile phones

Similar to cars, we're encouraged to buy the latest phone or upgrade every time a new model comes out. It's a phone, most apps are the same, there are limited differences but, like lemmings hurling ourselves off a cliff, as a nation we can't seem to stop ourselves from spending way too much on mobile devices. As with mortgages and cars, we're obsessed with the monthly payment, never the full cost. I did a quick internet search and found an Apple iPhone 14 Pro Max (the latest model at the time of writing) with 128GB capacity, 25GB data and unlimited minutes/texts at £42.99 a month and £199 downpayment. Over the two-year term, this works out at £1,230. Do you think this is good value?

I'm not a technophobe who still has a Nokia 3210; I have a Samsung Galaxy M31 (bought outright for about £200 in 2020) on a contract costing £4.95 a month (with a rolling one-month commitment) for unlimited calls and 5GB data. I have 11GB available from the 64GB storage and only ever had to top up usage data once. I will probably buy another Android in a few years, likely timed to coincide with Black Friday or another sale, and then resell my old phone on eBay. That said, always sense-check that the 'discounted sale price' is genuine, and not a marketing trick! I have Wi-Fi at home and most places I visit have it, so I don't consume that much data. I was looking around for a new contract for Lou's phone last year and from two major networks, the cheapest they offered when I gave them my usage and needs was £24/month and 20GB data. We ultimately bought a rolling monthly SIM for £7 and 6GB, much more in line with our usage. We're constantly being talked into overbuying rather than getting a contract that suits our needs.

If you don't have broadband at home and use your mobile data in its place, it might work out in terms of data usage but not the high capital cost of the phone. We recently took a trip to Iceland and were lucky enough to see the northern lights. They're particularly challenging to photograph but the latest iPhone would have taken better pictures. I took some reasonable photos for social media, so I wasn't too concerned about professional picture quality. Would I have paid £1,000 to get a couple of better photos? No.

When you're coming to the end of your contract, don't be tempted to upgrade. Have a look at your system settings, find out how much data you actually use and get a rolling one-month contract that matches your usage. Wait a year and with the savings, buy a 'last season' Android and keep on banking the difference. I have nothing against Apple; their iPhones are beautifully designed and have some great engineering features but I don't agree with the rate at which they roll out new models that are essentially the same and the marketing that encourages people to spend a premium on something that most don't really need. Iceland photography aside, Apple support is also excellent, and if you need it (and use it), then it's worthwhile. My 80-year-old aunt has an iPhone and regularly rings Apple to remind her how to do something, which is great, but I'm not aware that any of my friends with iPhones have ever used this service, but they're paying for the luxury of having it there.

Utilities

Pretty much all you need to do here is to use a price comparison website (many are listed on moneysavingexpert. com) but do keep track of when each contract is ending and, rather than waiting until the last minute, do some research to see if you can get a better deal in advance.

Insurance

Buying insurance is a bit of a gamble. You buy it because you want to be protected but equally hope you won't need to use it, so it's a sunk cost. I'd never skimp on house or car insurance but I tend to decline extended warranties or product insurance. Whatever insurance you take out, be clear about what's covered and that you're insuring at the right level. Again, comparison websites are a good resource.

Life insurance needs to be treated slightly differently. If you're employed, you often get 'death in service' as part of your pension, so you have an element of cover anyway. Just after we were married, we took out a £200,000 20-year joint life insurance policy, paying out in the event of one of us dying. It was principally to cover the mortgage and became useful down the line when remortgaging, as rather than taking the insurance included with the mortgage, we found it was invariably cheaper to arrange it independently.

If you do take out life insurance, you're likely to hit one of two scenarios. Coming to the end of your term, and in good health, you realise you've spent a load of money and got nothing for it. In our case it cost in total just over £5,000, and yes, I felt a little cheated. If you have an ongoing policy, the other option is when you hit 70 or thereabouts. You usually receive a letter saying your provider can continue to provide the same level of cover but your premiums will double. Alternatively, you can keep your premiums the same but the level of cover will be halved. This happens again at 75, 80 and so on. Basically, the odds of you dying are increasing and your cover is reducing or becoming prohibitively expensive. It's a horrible feeling, as you might stop the policy, drop dead tomorrow and you've wasted all that money; or you're enjoying good health, yet the cost of cover is ratcheting up.

As with critical illness cover, the decision to take out life insurance is a personal one. I'd suggest that, if you have dependents, it's a good idea to protect them if the worse should happen but if you don't need it, I wouldn't bother. We cancelled our life insurance policy after 18 years as we'd paid off the mortgage and didn't need the protection it offered (to pay off the mortgage), so we decided to write off the cost rather than continuing to pay premiums.

Cooking from scratch

Data from a 2022 YouGov survey suggests that the majority of Brits can cook, with only 12% classing themselves as poor chefs and 3% admitting to being 'very bad'. While 11% claimed to be 'very good', nearly half (47%) only rated themselves as 'fairly good', so there's potentially an opportunity to review the cost of eating, which is something we all do!

Cooking, and specifically cooking meals from scratch, is one of the key skills I acquired at university. We were a house of six and all put £20 in the kitty every month, taking turns once a week to cook a meal for the whole house. We also paid for bread, butter, toilet roll and milk out of the kitty, so it was feeding six for approximately £4. This figure does need adjustment for inflation but you get the gist. It taught me not only how to cook but what to cook, and how to create a filling, nutritious meal on a small budget. It also helped that I grew to love cooking and now do most of it at home. We still have meals cooked from scratch most days and minimise ultra-processed food and ready meals. It's a simple as going back to my parents' era (or more likely your grandparents, or even further back) – cook a roast chicken on Sunday with lots of vegetables, have risotto on Monday, make a pie on Tuesday and soup on Wednesday.

Also, you can forget most fancy kitchen gadgets: the two that offer the best value are a slow cooker (£20) and a stick blender (£15). They're cheap, readily available and low tech so rarely go wrong. If you're not great at cooking, don't buy expensive celebrity cookbooks. If you must, pick one up at a charity shop – there are always plenty. I have two large hardback Jamie Oliver books (presents, I didn't buy them) – and while they're lovely, the recipes are all available online. If you're not that confident, try cooking ingredient packs. We like Simply Cook but there are several others. It costs just over £10 a month and you choose four meal packs. You get the instructions and spices posted monthly and just need to add the basics – chicken, mushrooms, cream, pasta or potatoes, whatever. They are simple to follow (only a handful of steps and ready in less than 20 minutes) and it's easy to double up, add more base ingredients and bung some portions in the freezer. Lou says she can burn water but she can follow these, so I'm sure you can too. If you overindulge on takeaways, this is worth a try. You can get the family involved, you know what's gone into it, they're extremely tasty and more to the point you'll save money. Almost every week we have a 'freezer bingo' meal that we take out in the morning and microwave for an easy and quick dinner.

Aligned with learning to cook from scratch is to plan your food shopping. I know it's dull but every week, work out what you plan to eat, make a list of what you need and buy accordingly. Randomly picking up stuff from the shops on frequent trips leads to food waste (which equals money waste). We have a magnetic weekly grid stuck to the fridge and every weekend we jot down what we're doing and what we plan to eat. It doesn't matter if you don't stick to it 100% (we normally fail at least one day a week) but it really does help you plan. Only buy what you really need as well as making sure you actually use what you've bought.

Finally, a bit of brand awareness. Where do you shop? Again, it's not a new idea but try downshifting – from Waitrose to Sainsbury's or from Tesco to Aldi. Alternatively try supermarket-own brands – you'll be surprised at the similarity. And trust me, a lettuce is a lettuce. I should know, as one of my school holiday jobs was picking celery and lettuce at a local market gardener. We supplied the same lettuce to *all* the major supermarkets; the only one we treated differently was Marks & Spencer. They had a requirement that all lettuces should be above a certain weight. They would take all of them; we just had to segregate the underweight ones. However, they would spot check and weigh a sample of lettuces and if any failed, they'd reject the entire lorryload. So what did we do? If the weather had been poor and the next tranche of lettuce looked a little small, we watered it before picking, adding a few extra grams to each. So, I mean it, there's no difference in your supermarket lettuce but you might be getting a pre-washed one if you pay extra at M&S!

Loyalty cards

If you regularly use a particular retailer, make use of their loyalty programme if they have one. Tesco revolutionised this sector with the launch of their Clubcard way back in 1995, and most major retailers now offer something similar. While some offer more benefits than others, choose whatever's convenient for you. We use Lidl purely because there's one in town and the nearest big Tesco is ten miles away – it's not worth driving there just for the Clubcard.

Look out for other opportunities too; I travelled quite a bit with work and nearly always stayed in a Holiday Inn as I rated their loyalty programme, and we've had many free nights and upgrades out of it. Remember they are 'buying' your loyalty, offering you discounts or rewards so that you'll use them in preference to others. My only caveat would be don't be tempted to buy anything because you have a discount voucher – if you weren't going to buy it, don't buy it just because it's cheaper.

A slight twist on loyalty cards are cashback or affinity credit cards, which accumulate rewards against regular spending but aren't tied to a particular retailer. These can be great but you need to pick one you know you're going to use and have the flexibility to meet the terms and conditions of cashing in the rewards. Pre-Covid, we chose an airline affinity card as we knew we wanted to travel more and we've just bought first-class tickets to the Caribbean and only paid the airport taxes, saving us in the region of £5,000. So they're definitely worth it if you can be flexible with your travel dates – don't expect to be able to exchange them for cheap flights during the school holidays.

Discretionary spending

This means spending money on stuff you don't need to survive. You might think you need another pair of shoes but you probably don't. As with the previous section, if there's finance involved, you need to look at the total cost you're paying, the length of the agreement and how much interest or fees you're paying over and above the base cost of the item.

Technology and gadgets

As a society, in the UK I believe we're falling prey to increasing commercialism and 'greed' for many products, which is exacerbated by products that are replaced ever more frequently and with higher specifications or additional features. Although there are technological advances, many product releases don't really provide any real step-change in functionality over an older model, yet we're encouraged by marketing to replace technology before it fails. Additionally, some perfectly serviceable technology becomes obsolete when maintenance is no longer supported, in essence forcing you to upgrade to continue using it. Not only is this bad environmentally, it can also be a big drain on your finances.

Sorry to be a killjoy but I'd suggest you really don't need most of them, or at least you don't need the latest version!

If you're getting yourself out of a financial hole, hold back on anything that's not life critical and take at least a year to get yourself stable. Air fryers come into this bracket; they're marketed as the solution to the current energy crisis but in reality it's a marketing gimmick and you can do better than splashing out on yet another gadget that ends up in the cupboard under the sink. In the 1970s it was yoghurt makers (my parents bought one and used it twice) and I'll admit we also have a couple of relics in the kitchen that we don't really use – but nobody's perfect. However, I have been tempted, and recently bought an air fryer in the sales. I wasn't totally convinced but watched a TV documentary about them and together with a recommendation from a mate, I decided to try one. But don't pay more than £100; a reasonable one costs around £70. I recognised I could use it for chips from the freezer, crisping up jacket potatoes, salmon steaks, etc, and potentially use it once a fortnight in place of heating up our conventional fan oven and therefore saving a few quid. Time will tell how often we use it but at least I'll know I've not wasted more than £200 on a 'top of the range' model. But I'm still not convinced about cooking a full roast dinner for four in an air fryer. As for other gadgets, look around your home and see what you've previously bought, with all good intentions, and don't really use. Yes, I'm going to suggest selling them but in most cases you won't get much for them.

Clothes

This is a contentious one for many as clothes are very visible to others. Brands (or lack of a named brand) can lead to assumptions about the wearer, both positive and negative. They also provide us with a perception of 'feeling good' about ourselves. To be clear, I'm talking here about designer brands over regular store clothing. My challenge is whether a pair of designer jeans that cost three times as much as an own-brand pair from Next, for example, really is 'three times as good'? Will they last three times as long or be three times more comfortable? I still like to wear nice clothes, and by this I mean clothes that are comfortable and 'look good' on me (ie they fit well), but thinking about clothes as more of a functional purchase can save you a lot of money.

The trick is knowing which brands are worth it and which aren't. I'm a fan of Barbour as a robust outdoor coat, particularly as you can have it reconditioned and rewaxed (waterproofed) at a fraction of the cost of a new one, therefore it can last you 20 or more years, but sadly this is an exception. For most of our clothes, we apply a 'pound a wear' approach. Whatever you spend on an item of clothing, allocate a virtual £1 against the cost for every time you wear it. Once you've virtually 'paid yourself back' then it's OK to recycle (or sell, or give to charity) and replace it. For example, if you pay £20 for a nice work shirt and wear it two days a week for a year, you've got your value out of it. Another way of looking at it is to ask how much it costs you to wear. I needed a dinner jacket for a formal occasion and knew I wasn't going to use it that often. I couldn't find one second hand, so I bought one from Matalan for £100. Partly because I attend more charitable events these days, I've worn it (to date) 12 times, so just over £8 a wear. I have a couple more events coming up so this will improve, the only risk being that, having lost a bit of weight, it won't fit me – but I'll take that on the chin! And no one has ever made any comment that it doesn't look as good as one from Savile Row or with a well-known label inside.

It's one thing valuing what you buy and working out how often you use it but a slightly more important element is understanding whether a particular brand is anything special. After graduating, a friend of mine from university worked for a major textile company. She was seconded to north Africa where many of the garments were made. Much like contract manufacturing, several brands were made in the same factory, with the same machines and staff, with maybe a difference in material. At the time (in the late 1990s) we'd get a call every so often to say 'Give me your sizes, I'll bring some seconds'. We all duly drove across the country to try on what was available and if the clothes fitted and we liked them, we'd hand over £10 per item. The labels were crudely cut out but I bought a lovely dark grey Gieves and Hawkes suit, a cashmere blazer (believed to be Hugo Boss) and a Christian Dior blazer. I know it was Christian Dior as even though the label was chopped out, the branded lining gave it away. Fortunately, I'm still wearing these items and on current use I'm also now way below £1 per wear. So the moral of this story is, when it comes to brands, it's the marketing that tells you it's different but nine times out of ten, it's really not. Invariably, it's manufactured in the same factory as 'lesser' items.

It's also worth buying on reselling platforms. My current favourite is Vinted. While you might not get top dollar as a seller, there are bargains if you're a buyer. Since stopping work, I've started going to the gym again as I have more time, and I'd estimate about three quarters of people there wear branded clothing, with Nike and Under Armour the most common. It's also fair to say that many at my gym are not top athletes – they're regular people like me who just want to get a bit fitter. Those big brands are expensive and don't offer most gym-goers any advantage over cheaper brands other than how they feel wearing them. There's always the argument, particularly with shoes, that the more expensive trainers are better for your feet but aside from the fact that most high-end trainers never see a gym, I don't buy the argument. I do some running and have a pair of trainers made by a lesser-known brand. I tried several on before buying, but these fitted well and cost less than £40.

I do understand the allure of branded clothing and how it makes you feel better, irrespective of whether it's actually better quality – and I'm not totally immune to it myself. It's just that I refuse to pay the full ticket price for it – whether it be Vinted or TK Maxx, I'm much happier paying less than 50% of the list price than others who value the brand more highly. Therefore the three ways to reduce your spending on clothing are to challenge your perception of brands and whether they really offer good value, get good use out of your clothes – and if you can't resist some branded items, look at buying them when they're discounted.

The textile industry is also a major contributor to global emissions, particularly fabrics made from synthetic materials, which is increasingly common. According to 2017 research from WRAP (Waste and Resources Action Program), increasing the active life of all clothing by nine months would reduce the annual carbon, water and waste footprints of clothing by 20–30% each and cut resource costs by £5 billion, so it's not just your wallet that you're helping.

Other stuff you probably don't need

Technology is great. Some of the things you can do with it nowadays are truly amazing and the stuff of the science fiction of my childhood, when the most technically advanced gadget was James Bond's magnetic watch. The trouble is, we're building so much into products that we don't actually need, which increases cost and complexity and ultimately shortens lifespan. As an engineer at heart, I watched a documentary about building the new Land Rover Defender. The original Land Rover was a brilliant, functional design and lasted for decades. The narrator was talking about the new model and waxing lyrical about the new model's ability to drive through 90 cm of water, which, he assured us, was one of the key features that distinguished it from rivals. Not only this, but the wing mirrors have built in wading/depth sensors so you know how much of the 90 cm you're driving through. I would put money on the fact that none of the Defenders bought this year will ever use this facility, yet it's there and you've paid for it – approximately £85,000! I'm sorry if I'm starting to sound repetitive but it's time we woke up to the rampant consumerism we've got ourselves caught up in, which is the fault of those marketing departments (or 'the colouring-in departments' as Lou likes to call them). There's more insight into how they're hoodwinking you in a later chapter.

A word about functionality. Not only should you focus on buying the specification you need (ie functionality), you also need to be clear on the technical specification (the actual numbers) and if it does actually save you money. There's plenty of data relating to how much appliances cost to run. It's a straight calculation from the wattage or power rating of an appliance: at current electricity prices a 3kW kettle costs 17p for 10 minutes, a 2.1kW fan oven 71p per hour and a 1kW microwave 6p for 10 minutes. Our friend the air fryer comes in at around 30p per hour but the advantage over a conventional oven is that it also shortens cooking time as well as using less power. Let's say three hours for cooking a small roast chicken in the oven for £2.13 and in an air fryer one hour or 30p, giving you a saving of £1.83. If you've just fallen for the overspecified model at more than £200, you're going to have to cook 109 roast chickens to break even! Yes, it can cook other things too but you could also cook a lasagne or stew in the oven alongside the chicken so there are arguments for both. The fact remains that, as soon as you've bought your new gadget, the money's gone and will only slowly pay you back over a long period of time, assuming of course that you do actually use it as much as you tell yourself you will. It's not complicated maths but it often gets overlooked when looking at the glossy adverts. As I commented previously, a more economical bet would be a slow cooker at £20, which costs 5p per hour to use, so 30p would go you a chilli con carne or stew to feed four and a portion or two for the freezer – it's a no-brainer.

One positive thing to come out of the European Union is better labelling regarding energy efficiency on many appliances but you still have to do the maths to see if it's worth it. By all means buy a more efficient model (when you need to replace it) but make sure you understand the cost differential between an A- and C-rated fridge in terms of running costs. If it saves you £10 per year for the A-rated model, would it be worth paying £200 more for it than the C-rated one?

As with all big purchases, two common sense rules apply. First, look at where to buy it from as the cost can vary dramatically, particularly if there are different brands to choose from. Second, if you can, wait. Put it on a wish list and wait until there's a sale or until you've sold a couple of things on eBay to fund it. This second approach works for me, as I feel I've 'earned' whatever it is I'm buying (well, to be honest, I feel less guilty!) but invariably the urge to buy goes away and you realise you don't really need it after all. Of course, if something breaks and you need to replace it immediately, you can't wait – but don't skip doing a bit of research first. The TV in my office failed a while ago and as much as I love Amazon, I looked at several options and picked one up from Argos that afternoon, partly as I didn't want my TV being lobbed around parcel hubs. The price was comparable and, in this instance, convenience and speed were the winning factors.

Tattoos

Tattoos are another contentious issue but there's a reason why I'm including them, not least because they can be expensive, generally permanent and you can't sell them on like clothes! It would be easy for me to be flippant and say just don't do it but I'm not going to. Similarly, I could be accused of 'finger-wagging' or taking a pop at someone with an armful of tattoos, Oakley sunglasses, iPhone and AirPods, wearing Nike trainers and supping on a Starbucks – or, put another way, someone with a couple of thousand pounds' worth of visible discretionary spend.

However, my point is that, if it's large, a tattoo is a big expense, especially if you have several. I have nothing against them and even have a small one myself (Lou and I both got inked on our honeymoon) but I'd suggest thinking about when and why you're getting a tattoo, particularly an extravagant one. In my mind, it's a totally discretionary expense and therefore if you're prioritising your spend, it should be quite a long way down the list.

I've talked a lot about bigger purchases and we're now tailing into smaller stuff but it's important to cover off as they can build into a significant cost saving over time. Plus, it still follows the principle of changing your mindset about how you value purchases.

Over-the-counter medicines

This is another triumph for our friends at the colouring-in department. Every medicine sold has a product licence number (PL code), which shows the medical composition of the product. For example, OptiPharma Max Strength Cold and Flu capsules (Lidl, £1.99) and Benylin Cold & Flu Max

Strength capsules (B&M, £2.29) are differently branded and manufactured by different companies but the PL code is the same. It's the same tablet and will have the same effect. After a bit more research, I found the Benylin product listed in two well-known pharmacies for £3.79 and £4.20 respectively, so shop around. Don't be concerned about an unrecognised brand if the PL code is the same and don't assume that your local pharmacy is going to offer you the best value (although their medical advice will probably be better than what you'd get in Lidl!).

Although not a big ticket saver for many, I've included it to demonstrate a point. It's common for two similar products and in this case identical ones to be branded, marketed and sold at different prices. If you buy into this idea and are happy to accept the lesser-known brand, there are real savings to be made.

The lottery

Again, I wouldn't advise doing the lottery on a regular basis. If you buy a ticket for every draw, you can afford to put £25 in Premium Bonds every month. Use this as your emergency fund and you've still got the excitement of a bet, and you might well win a prize. The odds of landing a big payout with either are both slim, but as an added bonus of Premium Bonds, if you need to, you can take your money out again. What's not to like?

Lunch breaks

Aside from the obvious advice to avoid buying a daily coffee from Starbucks or Costa and a packaged sandwich, there's a link here to learning how to cook from scratch and getting better value from the food you buy. Another report by WRAP found that 70% of the annual food waste in the UK came from households and, according to data from the Office of National Statistics, the average UK household now spends around £3,234 annually on groceries, so there's a saving to be had. The second most common food waste is bread. Lou and I eat a fair amount of bread but never throw any away. Why? Because we keep it in the freezer! But back to lunch and sandwiches. Depending on what we have in the fridge, we often take out two frozen slices, butter them, add some ham, cheese or leftovers, make a sandwich, put it in a bag and pop it back in the freezer. When we were working or going out somewhere, we'd take one out in the morning and it would've defrosted by lunchtime. Not only does this save money and reduce waste, it's actually better for you as well. When the bread is defrosted, the starches present in fresh bread can't return to their original state and become less digestible. For most people, this is a good thing, as the higher proportion of 'resistant' starch means the once-frozen bread is digested more slowly by the body, causing a gentler blood sugar spike than fresh bread and potentially reducing the risk of type 2 diabetes. Dr Michael Mosley (2021) is also a fan of keeping his bread in the freezer and toasting it from frozen, one slice at a time: 'The resistant starch means fewer calories are absorbed by your body and therefore more are available for your microbiome [your gut bacteria], giving the "good" bacteria something to feed on and proliferate.'

Learn how to fix things

As opposed to throwing things away, which as you'll have gathered is a bit of a bugbear of mine, try to keep them for longer. Again, the internet is a fabulous resource for this and you'd be surprised how simple it is to fix some things. Our two-year-old microwave turntable stopped working a few months ago and I was reluctant to bin it. A quick Google search revealed several YouTube videos showing how to replace the motor underneath the turntable with just a screwdriver. This is when you realise that despite the brand on the outside, the insides are pretty much identical. We paid £6 for an exact replacement motor (delivered the next day from an online store) and the microwave lives to ping another day. Obviously don't tackle anything too serious or beyond your experience but many smaller failures can easily be fixed. Similarly, the catch on our washing machine door broke last week. It was surprisingly simple to take off the top (three screws), unscrew the broken lock, disconnect the little electrical sensor and replace it with a new one from eBay for £14. As with the microwave motor, it was the same part across many washing machine brands, irrespective of their 'rankings' in relation to perceived quality.

Summary

Spending less isn't just about finding the cheapest price. It's more about understanding value and buying the right specification (or not 'overbuying'). It's also about knowing the difference between needs and wants. You might need a car but you want a Mercedes. You might need a phone but you want the latest iPhone.

If you prioritise needs over wants earlier in life (and save money), you can then spend more freely on the wants later in life once you're more financially secure. We wanted to fly first class to the Caribbean, so we are. We wanted to buy a convertible, so we did. It's a matter of personal choice but we're happy to have skewed the balance this way and now we're reaping the rewards.

A BBC documentary I watched a while ago on how to pay off your mortgage in two years included an important takeaway about reducing your spending: you can only cut back your spending by so much. The flip side to this is how to earn more. I'll be looking at this in more detail in a later chapter after we've taken a visit to the colouring-in department.

Key takeaways

→ Review where you buy from and how – physical stores, delivery apps or online.

→ Keep things for longer and get more use out of them. Don't replace items for no reason.

→ Only buy the functionality you need; don't be tempted to buy a top of the range item if you don't need it or aren't going to use it.

→ Check your credit rating quarterly and if it's low, take steps to improve it.

→ Understand the true cost of buying on finance.

→ Overpay your mortgage whenever you can.

> *Because I'm worth it?*

Chapter 4

Understanding marketing and value

Marketing and value are often misunderstood – the former when it's done well and you believe what you see on a subliminal level; the latter because it's hard to accept that what you perceive to be 'good value' might not be... I believe the two concepts are linked and I'd define them as follows:

Marketing: the activity of presenting, advertising and selling a company's products or services in the best possible way.

Value: how much something is worth in currency or other goods for which it can be exchanged. An extension of this is how to value something, ie **evaluate** – to form an opinion of the amount, value or quality of something after thinking about it carefully.

As referenced earlier, the view that financial institutions are in business to make money, not solely to service you as a customer, extends to most things you buy. Obviously, there are staple products you must buy (food, clothing) but what you choose to buy is more often than not influenced by marketing. Of course, in some cases you have little choice or time and buy whatever's available but there's usually a selection to choose from. Our behaviour is often guided by marketing – either through direct messaging via television, newspapers or online; your previous experience with that retailer (reinforcing their marketing message) or peer pressure from your social circle or family. You'll often have a belief that one brand is better than another or trust that the retailer will offer you good value, irrespective of your knowledge of the product. Many of us might consider ourselves 'savvy' when it comes to marketing but we may not give too much thought to how marketing might have influenced our shopping habits and our decision making.

Branding

Brands will market or promote either low prices (such as the discount supermarkets Aldi and Lidl), product performance (BMW's 'the ultimate driving machine'), overall quality (Carlsberg's 'probably the best lager in the world') or value for money (John Lewis's 'never knowingly undersold'). You'll usually be drawn to one or two of these marketing styles over the others and this dictates the type of buyer you are and what you're tempted by. Recognising this in yourself helps you become more aware of the marketing that's being employed.

There are other mechanisms that embed a brand into our minds: a catchy jingle or strapline (such as 'We buy any car' or Ronseal's 'Does exactly what it says on the tin'), or a product endorsement by a celebrity. Despite the fact that everyone knows they're being paid to wear or use a particular product, many people believe that if it's good enough for the celebrity, it's good enough for them. This is even more true if you're a fan of that celebrity. There's a third, more niche, mechanism that could be summed up as 'user experience' – a good example being the lubricant and degreaser WD-40. Have you ever noticed the smell? It's slightly sweet and unlike other similar products. The exact formula of WD-40 is a trade secret but, having worked in the business, my money is on it being a simple fragrance that has little to do with the product's lubricating properties. However, when you use it, nine times out of ten it does what it's intended to do and you associate that success with the smell. Therefore, WD-40 becomes your 'go-to' trusted brand when you need a spray lubricant. Even though there are others on the market, you don't look at them.

Understanding value

Marketing therefore exists to tell you (or convince you) to buy something by promoting a particular attribute. Over time, you become loyal to a particular brand and continue to buy those products because you trust them to give 'good value' and don't need to spend time looking for alternatives. This is the marketeer's dream: you're hooked on the product or retailer and they know they can continue to sell you stuff as you've bought into that brand. It's important to note here that I'm not saying these products are no good or won't perform, but are you really getting 'good value'? To understand this, you need to look at what value is and the right level to buy at. This is important because, in general, a brand that's perceived as 'higher quality' is more expensive but I'm convinced it doesn't mean it's any better value or that a product from a 'lesser' brand will perform any worse. In essence, I'm saying that many of us are tempted to buy a higher-end brand than we really need and that means we're overspending.

Ask yourself what 'value' you need a particular product

to have. Again, this might be different for all of us. How often you use a product, how long it will last and how many of the features it has (that you will use) all contribute to what level of value is right for you.

I love shopping and understand the excitement of owning something new. And, despite my overall tendency not to waste money, I'm sometimes tempted to buy branded items or things I don't really need. However, I've managed to control this habit by only purchasing a handful of branded items and generally only buying second hand or in a sale. My desire not to pay over the odds for something is usually stronger than wanting any particular item but I'm not immune to the odd lapse. It's interesting that my dislike of wasting money has grown stronger in proportion to the growth in value of the investments from those savings.

The questions to ask yourself here are:

1. Do I need all that functionality and will I use it?
2. Is it really any better than a similar product, irrespective of the label?
3. Do I believe it will have a reasonable lifespan (ie at least five years)?

Then it's down to a financial choice of whether you're prepared to pay a price premium for a particular brand over a lower-priced brand. There's often a final option of whether the branded item is available second hand, so you can get the 'brand experience' at an unbranded price. This is particularly true of cars but also of clothing. As I've mentioned, I'm a big fan of the online marketplace Vinted, not only to resell unwanted items but also to buy good quality clothes. I'm amazed by how many items for sale are 'new with tags', for a fraction of the cost of buying them from the retailer. In the past few months, Lou has bought an unworn Barbour jacket and a pair of new/boxed leather boots by Dune and I've bought a pair of unworn Next leather loafers – all at less than a third of the price of the shop-bought versions.

As I've said before, managing your money doesn't just mean being ultra frugal all the time; you're allowed to indulge in a bit of 'brand luxury' every so often. But it's important not to lose sight of the concept of value and changing your spending habits to focus on products that do represent good value.

Seven brand tiers

How, then, do you determine what *is* good value versus overpriced or too cheap? Consider the following seven brand tiers.

1. A **niche brand** that only makes or sells a specific type of product and is a market leader. Their focus is on one product type – for example, Rolex or Rolls-Royce.

2. A **designer label**: many clothing brands fit into this category. A shirt is a shirt; the design may vary slightly or use different materials but it does the same functional job as every other shirt. Generally, the designer label is considered a premium brand and therefore at the upper end in terms of cost (to buy). Originally, these were the big fashion houses such as Versace or Christian Dior, who crafted small runs of bespoke, often hand-made, clothing, but it has moved into more mainstream production where the name is heavily marketed but the manufacture is no longer particularly unique, nor the design anything special. I would also

include instances where a brand is used across an alien product range. For example, Porsche build cars and if I were after a sports car, it would be one I'd consider. They don't make watches, so I wouldn't buy a Porsche-branded watch; I'd buy a watch from a company whose business is making watches.

3. A **supermarket brand**: functional (everyday) products that carry a retailer's own brand labelling but are similar to other products. All the big supermarkets have these, as well as large retailers such as John Lewis or Screwfix.

4. A **'boring' brand**: it does the job, isn't overly expensive or exciting but just doesn't have much in the way of street cred. These types of brands are often shunned due to peer pressure. These brands might be thought of as mid-range – neither perceived as high quality but equally not seen as budget nor cheap. They are normally related to long-term businesses, not newly formed start-ups. I'd put Vauxhall cars, Clarks shoes and Bic biros in this category.

5. A **duplicate brand**: this type of brand was originally seen in the car industry but is becoming more widespread in other markets. Volkswagen's own brands range from Bentley and Audi through to VW, Škoda and Seat. In essence, they share much of the 'internals' of the product and benefit from shared support services in design, purchasing, supply chain, etc.

6. A **pseudo brand**: this type of brand is often historic and was previously successful but the underlying business has struggled and been bought out by another retailer. House of Fraser

is a good example of this, having snapped up many traditional brands such as Slazenger, Everlast, Jack Wills, Evans Cycles, Gieves & Hawkes and many more. They're recognisable names but are no longer independent.

7. An **'unknown' brand**: regularly seen in online marketplaces with products that look similar to branded items but are produced by companies with more consonants in their names than a bad round in *Countdown*.

You may have concluded that tier 1 is the most expensive and tier 7 the least expensive. I'm using the word expensive carefully here to mean the price the customer pays. Aside from tier 1, the manufacturing cost (ie the effort taken to make the product) is broadly similar. There's also the cost of the raw material and this does vary, notably for clothing and food. Clothing is straightforward: silk is more expensive than polyester, leather more expensive than plastic. Food is a little more complicated as most of us don't have any technical knowledge about ingredients but it follows a trend of cost reduction. When I was a kid in the 1980s, Jacob's Club biscuits were advertised with the jingle 'If you like a lot of chocolate on your biscuit, join our club'. However, as the cost of cocoa soared, they reformulated the ingredients to include more fats, emulsifiers, sweeteners and flavourings (all cheaper) instead of cocoa, to the point where they might no longer be truly what we might think of as chocolate biscuits, but labelled as having a 'chocolate-flavoured coating'. Although they were at the same price point and branded as the same biscuit, they had become a lesser-quality product. While this type of reformulation occurred with many food products, the current trend is to move back to more natural ingredients; indeed, McVitie's Club

Orange Chocolate Biscuit now cites 'no hydrogenated vegetable oil, and no artificial colours or flavours' in its ingredients.

Leaving aside tier 1 items, as these are placed at the luxury end and not really considered everyday nor frequent purchases, the concept of 'shifting down a brand' is often cited as a way of saving money (swapping your regular purchase to a 'lower brand' but getting a product of very similar quality and greater value) and I wouldn't disagree with this. It's particularly true in relation to supermarket or large retailer brands or those companies with multiple, duplicate brands.

A value or brand choice?

Early in our careers, when Lou and I worked for the same company, we were both offered a company car at the same time. We had different jobs but were at the same level and had the same budget. Lou chose a 1.6 petrol VW Golf hatchback and I chose a 2.0 diesel Škoda Octavia estate. Comparing the two cars, mine had the higher specification: climate control over air conditioning, leather over cloth seats and a more powerful and economical engine. But inside the car, aside from the badge and a few minor details, it was exactly the same – the same door handles, dashboard dials and switchgear. You'd be hard pressed to spot the difference, yet the perception of the brands was very different and I got a lot of stick from friends and colleagues for driving a Škoda. At the same time, one of the account managers chose an Audi A4 saloon from the same price bracket. Although perceived as a higher quality brand, he had to contend with wind-up windows and couldn't afford metallic paint or alloy wheels! As a side note, when I left the company and handed back the car, they ran it as a pool car for a further six years. Proof, if needed, that it was a value for money decision.

With an understanding of how brands are marketed as well as downshifting brands, I'd also recommend shopping in the middle tiers (3 to 6). I'd avoid the 'unknown brand' unless the frequency/price ratio is low enough that you'd consider it a throwaway item rather than something you'd want to last for a reasonable period of time. This frequency of use is related to an earlier concept in the previous chapter, or £/use as a mechanism of evaluating the cost of an item against how many times you're going to use it. In this case, the argument is that if you're going to use something often, then it's worth buying a better quality product rather than something cheap and cheerful that might not last as long. However, don't confuse better quality with higher price; seek to understand the underlying quality of the product, not what the marketing hype is telling you.

Raw material cost, performance and product quality

So how do I know that less well-known brands are often just as good as other, better-known brands? It comes from spending many years working in manufacturing and distribution/retail where I learned how contract manufacturing operates. Some of you might be familiar with the 'biscuit argument'. Most supermarkets sell an own brand version of, say, Rich Tea biscuits, so there are maybe a dozen variations. They're often made in the same factory, perhaps with a small tweak to the ingredients and of course the outer wrapper. But the production line, the ovens, the temperature control, hygiene standards, mixing bowls, quality checks, packing and storage are all the same, leading to very similar end products. While many will argue that you can't beat the original McVitie's or Waitrose Rich Tea, in taste tests there's often little difference to those from Tesco or Aldi. Added to this, there's always personal taste and a preference for one over another, so there will never be a universally agreed 'best product'.

Now we get onto the technical make-up of products – the core ingredients and how they influence performance. One company I worked for had an own brand range of maintenance aerosols (lubricating oils, degreasers, cleaners, etc) and one year we decided to relaunch it with a new can design so that the sales team had a 'new, improved' product to sell. We were already using a contract manufacturer, so we agreed a funky new can design and had meetings to discuss what we could change in the formulae to be able to claim the products were indeed 'new and improved'. One product was a graphite spray (a lubricant), which we tweaked a little and sent samples out to the sales team for customers to test. The feedback was universal – it was rubbish and worse than the old one. We hadn't changed much and couldn't understand the reaction but after a discussion with the manufacturer, they pointed out that the new product was clear and suggested that some people might not associate this with graphite. We tweaked it a little more and sent out the new samples, only to get a similar universal response, albeit a totally different one, which was 'excellent' and 'so much better than the last lot'. What had we done? We'd added some black dye to the product. It was technically no different (in terms of lubrication) but the customer perception was that this was a good quality graphite spray and we even managed to increase the price of this new, improved version.

With aerosols, it's sometimes not just the active ingredients, it's what else makes the product work – this time, brake cleaner. To understand this, you need to know how aerosols work; there's the can (obviously), the active ingredients, compressed air and a product known as the carrier or propellant – generally a liquified gas that the active ingredients are mixed with to make the product spray out of the nozzle without clogging. Typically, a good brake cleaner has a powerful spray that gets the active ingredient onto the surface you're trying to clean, so for this product we increased the percentage of compressed air and propellant, the two cheapest ingredients. Again, we received excellent feedback that the new product was 'way better' than the old version and 'literally blasted away brake dust', when all we'd done was effectively reduce the amount of active ingredient in the product to reduce the cost. This time, we kept the selling price the same but increased our margins as well as increasing overall sales volume since it was seen as a top-performing product.

I'm sharing these two examples to demonstrate that product quality isn't defined solely by the brand or the manufacturer and that often an unbranded (or a brand with a lower perceived quality) product might well be just as good. It goes back to the basic concept that any company is in business to make money; it buys or makes a product for a certain cost and has to sell it to the customer at a higher price to make a profit and thus sustain its business. If a company is spending a lot on marketing, it must either sell it at a higher price for the same 'quality' of product, or make it at a lower cost, at the risk of lower product quality. So when you're buying a higher branded product, you need to think about how much of that purchase price you're prepared to pay for the actual product and how much of it is purely funding the marketing or celebrity endorsement.

Brand reputation

At the other end of the scale, there are the completely unknown and unrecognisable brands, typically seen listed in online marketplaces and often at the lowest price against comparable products. I'm not a fan of these unless you're making a disposable one-off purchase. Despite what I've said above about managing product cost, there's a limit to how far you can trim cost and margin without compromising product quality. The adage 'if it sounds too good to be true, it probably is' fits here. Plus, there's often no reputation behind the brand and no guarantee of longevity of supply. I believe it's important to buy from a trusted retailer or a brand you know because you'll have additional recourse if the product fails. A larger brand will more likely support you with better aftercare – and this is true of all those middle brands from the list above; it's just the complete unknowns I'd steer clear of, despite the lure of a cheap price.

Of course, I'm not infallible and also get tempted by a bargain. I was looking for a carry-on rucksack for a flight and didn't want to spend a huge amount as I wasn't a regular flyer. I chose cheap – two for £16 online; they looked OK when they arrived and we duly set off on holiday. While walking through Tenerife airport, one of the straps tore away, so I went back online to see that the product was 'no longer available' so it wouldn't have been much help to others to leave a review of what I'd experienced. When I contacted customer services, the seller was a distribution company that at least offered a partial refund. After all, the strap could be re-sewn and Lou's was still intact. Although the retailer covered the poor quality, I was annoyed with myself that I'd fallen into the trap of buying 'too cheap'. As the saying goes, 'buy cheap, buy twice' and this is true of the bottom end of the market.

Technology

There's one product category that you also need to be careful with and that's technology. Primarily this is down to Moore's Law, which states that the number of transistors on a microchip doubles every two years, which in layman's terms means we can expect the speed and capability of our computers to increase every two years, yet we'll pay less for them. The challenge here is that product lifespan is getting ever shorter and we're being encouraged to buy the latest version each time it's launched, when the existing model is still doing a reasonable job. Part of the marketing approach here is to include an element of built-in obsolescence (typically by not providing technical support for older models) and part is down to Moore's Law itself: for example, if you have 25 apps installed on your phone, it might start off being well within the available storage. As apps are developed, more functionalities generally require more space and as these are updated you may find that, after a year or two, the storage required by your 25 apps now exceeds what's available. It's good practice to keep apps updated rather than saving space by not updating them, so you end up needing a new phone with more capacity just to stand still.

While I love technology, I do have a challenge with this shorter lifespan and the near constant push to replace perfectly serviceable products ever more frequently. Coming back to financial management, if you fall into the trap of investing in too much technology too often it's a potentially huge drain on your personal finances. It would be unrealistic of me to try to convince you to shun all technology but as with other themes in this book, if you want to take control of your finances, you need to challenge yourself with the question, 'Do I really need this?'

Twenty years ago, Lou bought me a watch as a wedding present – a Seiko Kinetic (self-winding) – for about £150, which tells me the date and time. I've worn it every day and had it serviced once to replace the internal battery, so in today's terms, it's an investment of approximately £300. Looking online today, a series 8 Apple iWatch is around £400 and I'd put money on whoever buys one will not be wearing it in three to four years' time, let alone 20. Of course, it's your money to spend however you like but I'm hoping to give you some insight into how to value your money (and your spending) so that you have more confidence in planning a more stable financial future.

That's not to say I'm immune to making decisions that don't work out, at least from a financial perspective. About ten years ago, I bought a digital SLR camera. It cost about £400 and I've taken some great pictures with it but my phone (at around £200) now takes better photos and, more to the point, is always with me and fits in my pocket. Looking on eBay, I'd struggle to sell the camera for £50. Frustrating as this is, we can't all be perfect at predicting how technology will develop. I just try not to let it happen too often and, more often than not, I'm not an early adopter of any new technology, preferring to wait until it matures.

Behavioural biases and quality perceptions

To wrap up this section on marketing and value I'd like to share a couple of examples to show how positioning a price (or discount) can influence our decision to buy, separate from product 'quality'. I'm not going into detail about all the various pricing strategies but Figure 6 demonstrates a couple of examples of behavioural biases from Dan White of Smart Marketing; they nicely demonstrate how positioning the price of a product influences how we perceive its 'value' and therefore whether we're prepared (or convinced) to buy it. I remember an old sitcom from my childhood, *Terry and June*, where the hapless Terry bought a new TV because it had 50% off. He tried to reason with his wife that the discount meant he'd saved £20. And since the TV now only cost £20, it was effectively free. We might laugh at the absurdity of this logic but as the table demonstrates, our brains can be misled.

The power of free: people don't like 'cheap' but they love 'free'	
Two bars of chocolate; priced at 1p and 15p – 73% will choose the 15p bar. The penny bar is considered inferior.	Same two bars, dropped in price by a penny, 69% now choose the free bar over the 14p one.
Rule of 100: we perceive discounts differently on products costing more or less than £100	
On a £1,000 TV, £200 off sounds more attractive than 20% off, yet it's the same amount.	While on a £10 shirt, 20% off is more attractive than £2 off.
Framing effects: highlighting a positive attribute makes a product more attractive	
75% lean minced beef is seen more positively than advertising 25% fat.	Rather than quoting a vehicle's poor 20mpg economy, say that it's best in its class.

Figure 6: Behavioural biases (source: Dan White, smartmarketing.me)

So what am I really saying about marketing? You might think I don't hold that profession in particularly high regard; while I love some of the creativity, I'm not keen on the underlying idea of trying to sell you something that you don't really need. Making your buying decision purely based on function would in many cases reduce what you spend. Due to the way manufacturing technology has advanced and the development of larger, global supply chains, what used to be considered a premium, high-quality, low-volume product has become mainstream. Brands have retained their premium tag but they are now more mass market. For example, when I was growing up, the best-selling car was the Ford Cortina, which sold millions. Much less common was the BMW 3-series, with the early two-door models giving 1970s junior management 'a chance to enjoy a prestigious badge and a touch of exclusivity'. For the price of a Cortina 2.0 Ghia in 1977 (around £4,000) you could have had an entry-level BMW 316 – a car that was smaller, more basic and less powerful. About ten years ago, I drove a Mondeo, the successor to the Cortina, and at the time, more people drove a BMW 3-series than a Mondeo; I was now driving the 'rarer' car, while the BMW had become mainstream. I'm not saying it's not a great car – it is, and I have one – but it has now lost that 'premium exclusivity' that it once had, while retaining the price premium.

There's also a variance between perceived and actual quality. *What Car?* magazine regularly lists the most unreliable cars, usually peppered with premium brands such as Porsche, Audi and Range Rover, so I'd contend that many are not basing a buying decision on functionality and true quality. When I took in my BMW for its first MOT, I was told my three-year manufacturer's warranty had expired. My previous Vauxhall Insignia came with a lifetime 100,000 warranty, and I ran the car for six years and 125,000 miles. The BMW is arguably perceived as the 'better quality' brand but the warranty the manufacturer provides suggests otherwise. (For the record, the only thing replaced under warranty on the Vauxhall was a boot strut, so I can confirm it was solidly built.)

Go on, treat yourself

Finally, buying things that give you a bit of a 'high' and make you feel good about yourself are often associated with certain brands, and this can't be ignored. But it's independent of what you're actually buying, so you have to acknowledge this impact if you're reflecting on your shopping behaviours and habits. Psychotherapist Pamela Roberts (from the Priory Group) sums this up better than I can: 'Society promotes the positive effects of shopping as beneficial – "give yourself a treat", "what you need is some retail therapy". We are exposed to highly sophisticated marketing techniques. It is easy to see how this, together with the very real, if short lived, psychological benefit and "easing" from stress or emotional pain that making a purchase can bring, is for some akin to the short-term benefits of substances.'

Ultimately, by understanding and managing your 'brand spending', you can spend less. If you then use those extra savings to invest in your future by paying a bit more off your mortgage or investing a little more in your pension, you'll have started on the journey to making better decisions that will put you in a more stable financial position. Not only this, but by overcoming the marketing and peer pressure to buy more expensive brands, it will give you the confidence to be your own person, make your own decisions and ultimately have more confidence that you're spending your money wisely.

Let me share one final example that shows how the perception of value can vary. Many years ago, a friend of mine ran a rally car as a hobby and I helped with servicing the car at events. One Christmas, as a thank you, he gave me a Snap-on ratchet screwdriver. It's a well-known brand with a great reputation and became my go-to tool whenever I was doing DIY. I'd go as far as to say I loved it and yes, using it made me feel good! Last year, the ratchet mechanism broke and while I was looking to replace it, I recalled that Snap-on tools had a lifetime warranty. So I sent a message via the US website, explained the problem and waited. To be honest, I wasn't expecting much. Two days later the local agent phoned me and arranged to pick it up. They repaired it and returned it to me two days later – at no cost. The customer service was fantastic and I didn't hold back on sharing how excellent the brand was, even on social media. However, an old colleague commented that it was a £100 screwdriver and it had broken, so was it really that good? They fixed it for free but perhaps you'd have expected it not to break in the first place. There's no right or wrong answer here. Would I have spent £100 on a screwdriver in the first place? Probably not. So I'll admit, it's complicated.

Key takeaways

→ Marketing exists to get us to buy something – whether we need it or not.

→ Think about function and specification – what do you actually need and what attributes of the product do you actually value?

→ What used to be premium has become mainstream. This doesn't mean premium brands have dumbed down; mainstream products have generally upped their game across the board but without the price hike.

→ Don't ever feel ashamed of what you buy. People really don't notice or care as much as you think they might. Be confident in your spending.

→ By all means treat yourself every so often and buy whatever 'luxury' brand you want but keep it as an infrequent treat, not the norm.

Chapter 5

How to earn more

There are a number of ways to earn money alongside your main employment. When you think of earning more, consider it as 'gaining wealth' – in which case you can include pensions, investments, income from property or doing something else that generates income. This final option is often referred to as a 'side hustle' and is commonly misreported in the media and various internet platforms as a miracle 'get rich quick' scheme but, like so many things you read online, the reality is far from the truth. There are no guaranteed, highly paid side hustles that work for everyone (or even work for most people) but there are some things you can do to generate additional income. I'll highlight a couple and explain why I don't think they should be your main focus. From a career perspective I will cover those in full-time employment on PAYE (pay as you earn) taxed income, as my experience is mostly with this model. I'll touch on the self-employed model but it's not my area of expertise. However, much of the advice about your career is transferable to self-employment, contract or other fields of work.

When I was a student, I remember having a chat with one of my friends who'd finished university and was then a graduate accountant. His advice has stuck with me ever since: 'Aim to earn £1,000 for every year of your life.' Therefore, at 25, aim to earn £25k; at 40, £40k, and so on. I'm not sure if this stacks up with inflation but like all good metrics, it's simple and long lasting. I've used it throughout my career and even though I didn't always meet the criteria, the ethos was there. Whether it was via a bonus or pay rise, promotion or moving jobs, it gave me a focus of 'continual improvement' in salary that has helped our financial stability. It was an aspirational metric as well, because when I started my working life at 22 I was earning around £10,000, so I clearly had a lot of catching up to do! This ethos instils the concept of career progression – how to help you get a pay rise, what you can for the best chance of promotion or, if you've hit a ceiling at your current company, how you can secure a new job and a step-change in salary. If I'm honest, I haven't followed this as aggressively as you might think, as I'm naturally a little lazy and much prefer the status quo. Most of my job changes have been forced upon me but the concept was always in the back of my mind and it's helped me to manage my career upwards.

Later on, I also took advice from my sister (who has been considerably better paid than me) after I told her I'd received a £1,000 bonus that year and was clearly very happy with it. She was less impressed and told me to focus on increasing my base salary, as that was a year-on-year increase, not a one-off. Thinking of your salary as a pizza and your pay rise as a slice, if you're always going to get the same percentage slice, aim to increase the size of the pizza! While I didn't always achieve this, the idea to continually increase my base salary was there.

Before we start, I need to dispel the idea that I've had a stellar career, regular bonuses or pay rises and was highly paid. While researching this book, I realised I only had a pay rise about every other year and even then, only 1–2% or sometimes less than that. I've had a few bonus payments but that's all. Yes, I've been paid well, but not as much as many of my peers. Of course, a great salary and a regular pay rise would be fantastic but realistically this isn't always going to happen, as some companies have rigid structures and pay scales. The right mindset is to start to think about the options you have to increase your salary and then work towards them. It might be an additional qualification, taking on more responsibility or a larger team, changing companies, or even changing career.

Some career advice

I don't know about you but in my day most people had their last real piece of 'career advice' at school, just after their O-levels or A-levels, as exams were known then. I grew up in an environment where university was the logical next step after school (despite neither of my parents going to university, I'm forever grateful to them for encouraging me to go). In terms of what I wanted to pursue as a career, that was even more vague; I was practical and good at design and technology, so engineering seemed like a good bet. In reality, I've received very little in terms of career guidance, although a pearl of wisdom from my godfather did stick in my mind. He suggested I should always be on the lookout for my next job. Actually, his exact words were 'You have the luxury of your current company paying you while you decide where you want to work next.' If anything, I probably learned more from my mentoring role at Amazon and guiding the careers of others than from any advice that has ever been given to me. This chapter covers what I've learned.

One of my early mentees showed an aptitude for technology and, as I needed some help with modernising the IT infrastructure, I took him on after his apprentice year. He was fantastic, a quick learner with new technology, and he was soon much more technically capable than I was. We were chatting one day and he asked why he was paid less than me when he knew more about our network and how it functioned. The answer was simple: I had A-levels, a degree and more experience, while he'd left school at 16 with very few qualifications. A few weeks later we came back to the subject and he asked if he could have some time off work (an afternoon per week) to enrol at a local college, which I supported. After a year, he had his first qualification under his belt. Then the crunch discussion came – he figured there was little career progression available where he was, so he concluded that he'd have to find another job with more opportunities. I was gutted to lose him but it was the right decision. I kept in touch after he'd left and supported his bold decision a few years later to take some time out from work to undertake a residential course and acquire his Microsoft certification.

A few years later, he asked me for a reference, which I gave, saying I'd have no hesitation to hire him again if I had the opportunity. The following day I received a very excited call from him, thanking me as he'd been offered a job in the Cayman Islands. It was a fantastic opportunity, which he grasped with both hands. He spent a successful few years there, met his future wife and returned to the UK to his current position as a senior solutions architect for a large PLC. The moral of this tale is that even from a low starting point, you can still build a successful career. Of course, you have to have some good luck along the way but ultimately it's down to you to make things happen, have the courage to address the areas you need to improve and the confidence to promote yourself.

I came across this quote recently that resonated with my approach: 'In every job you should either be earning or learning – preferably both.' If you're not gaining skills or experience that will land you that next job, or if you're not earning a wage that meets your needs, you need to find another job. I know it's not always as simple as just saying 'find another job' and there have been times when I've been unemployed and not been able to find anything for many months – but you have to maintain a positive approach and proactively try to manage your career as opposed to sitting back and waiting for it to happen. I'm a big fan of the professional networking site LinkedIn, partly because it's a rich hunting ground for jobs but also because it's a free advertisement for you and your skills, which is particularly helpful to recruiters when they're searching for candidates. I'd also suggest regularly reposting or sharing posts that are pertinent to your industry and commenting on them in a way that shows you're knowledgeable and interested in your work.

There are also other traits that will help you stand out, which don't need any qualifications or skills, such as being punctual, your work ethic, your body language and attitude in meetings, being open to coaching and volunteering for something when no one else wants to do it. The key here is that you're not just a 'face in the crowd' or a 'name on a page'; your management will at some point be looking to develop or promote someone and you want to be that someone they think of first. Amazon manages its hiring and promotion on 'leadership principles', which are used across the board, at all levels and in every department. I like this transparency and the idea that you're looking to develop people with certain traits and attitudes over pure qualifications, levelling the playing field for your personal development. Of course, it's not guaranteed to work all the time and not all management structures and companies are perfect – but what have you got to lose?

However, make sure to check that your good nature isn't

being taken for granted. Many professional roles run over the standard 40-hour week and every so often it's useful to benchmark where you are in terms of 'true salary'. Let's say you're earning £40k a year and working five eight-hour days with two weeks' holiday. That's £20 for each hour worked, before taxes and National Insurance. If you find yourself regularly staying late in the office or catching up on emails over the weekend, you're actually doing 50 hours a week, so you're really only on £16 for each hour worked. That means you'd be on £32,000 a year at this rate on a 40-hour week, which doesn't sound so attractive. So if you're disproportionally losing out on your free or family time, be wary of believing you're on a great salary. If you're happy with the salary and work/life balance, that's fine, but the point is that your pay might not be reflecting what you're truly worth and there's an opportunity to change that by increasing your pay base or reducing your hours.

However, there have been many times in my career when I've had positive feedback in reviews about the fact that I was prepared to do extra work or take on something outside my remit. This brings up the subject of reviews, whether formal or informal. I was shy as a child and naturally quite passive, so I understand that being assertive with your boss can feel daunting. I don't know what gave me the courage to ask for a pay rise to secure my first mortgage but it worked and perhaps helped to build my confidence in my later career. The result was definitely a one-off but the approach of being assertive with my personal objectives has stayed with me. Ultimately, you're working to get paid and you want to either be paid more or get more recognition. Your company won't have unlimited opportunities, so it's a good idea to frame these discussions with questions that help you get where you want to be, for example:

- What opportunities are there for me to improve my skills as a people manager?
- What could I have done differently this year?
- I really want to be promoted to the ABC team, so what should I focus on to achieve that?

These are often difficult discussions to have and if you're not getting great answers or support, then the solution is to start looking for a role in another company where you can make progress.

On the subject of driving progress, here's a final thought on the value of qualifications. A few years ago there were big supply chain delays across post-Brexit Europe and a shortage of HGV drivers. My European boss was talking to her son and encouraging him to revise hard for his exams so he could go to university. His response was, 'Why? I could take the HGV test and earn €70,000 driving a lorry.' He wasn't wrong and if it's right for you, that's great – you don't need necessarily need academic qualifications unless you want to go down a particular career path. My cousin drives HGV tankers and earns a very nice living – or used to, as he and his wife have just rented out their house for 18 months and set off on a round-the-world tour. The beauty of that is, when he returns, if he wants to, he can pick up work at the same rate. Similarly, one of our tenants is a successful landscape gardener with no formal qualifications – proof that success isn't about whether you have a degree or not but what's right for you and how you manage your career.

An introduction to pensions

Pensions normally go hand in hand with your career, particularly if your employer contributes. But irrespective of that, there's one simple reason why pensions are in this section –

you can earn free money via the government's tax break. For every contribution you make, the government will add 20% (40% if you're a higher-rate taxpayer). The only downside is that you can't access it until you're 55 (at the time of writing). But having a savings scheme that prevents you dipping into it is no bad thing. In essence, it ensures that your money is invested for a longer period of time, so the earlier you start, the better. A popular quote relating to investments is 'It's not timing the market, it's time in the market that counts.' This means that over a long time, investments are more likely to perform better (make more money) than trying to time buying an investment at a low price and selling at a higher one.

To underline this point, I'll use an example of twin brothers with different investment strategies. One invests £10,000 a year from the age of 25, together with matched company contributions – but stops paying when he's 40. He has personally invested £150k. His brother starts later in life and saves the same £10,000 a year from age 35, matched by his employer all the way through to retirement at 65 – 30 years in total and a personal investment of £300k. Assuming a 6% return on investment (not taking account of inflation), the first brother's investment would be worth £1,058,912 when he was 65. However, the second brother's investment would be worth only £838,019 at 65. Just let that sink in for a moment; the first brother invested £150,000 *less* but has an investment worth £220,893 *more* and the only difference is that he started investing earlier.

Together with the tax benefit from the government and employer contributions, pensions are a huge lever in gaining wealth, so you should plan to start saving into a pension as soon as possible. Previously, company pensions have been 'opt in' (you have to specifically join a scheme if there is one) but the legislation has now changed to being 'opt out', where you're automatically enrolled, which is better. You can also benefit from pension tax breaks if you're self-employed (via a limited company); if you're not employed, you can still invest £2,880 into a pension each year, with tax relief taking this to £3,600. This is particularly useful if you're in a relationship and one of you doesn't work, perhaps because of childcare. Employer contributions also vary considerably, particularly between the public and private sectors. In their 2022 report, the Institute for Fiscal Studies reported that public sector (employer) contributions were an average of 18% in 2021, against the private sector growing more slowly to just under 6% for the same period. I would have loved an 18% contribution – working in the private sector meant that typically my employer contributions were in the 3–5% range but it still helped to build a solid pension pot that has contributed to us being able to retire earlier.

Buying and renting property

Property is the third big-ticket lever that will help to increase your wealth. While not ignoring the fact that getting onto the property ladder is a significant challenge for many these days, particularly in the recent climate where interest rates (and therefore mortgage repayments) are significantly higher than they have been for the past ten or so years, buying a property will likely be your single biggest investment and therefore it's always going to be hard. However, it's a lesson that interest rates can go up and a potential increase needs to be considered when you take out any mortgage deal. As I referenced earlier, I can remember talking to my dad in the late 1980s when interest rates were at 14% and Lou and I were hit with rates rising to more than 8% on our mortgage in the late 1990s. It's likely to be one of your biggest monthly outgoings and that's why I believe so strongly in it being a top priority. Putting this to one side, you can leverage money from property in other ways too.

In a similar vein to the cost of frequent remortgaging mentioned in an earlier chapter, physically moving is also expensive. Costs such as solicitors, removals, redecorating or buying new furniture can amount to several thousand pounds, so it makes sense to try to minimise how often you move. I appreciate that there are many reasons to move (for example, a growing family or a change of job) but aiming to buy a house for the longer term is a smart move.

I had many conversations with my parents about my first house as I was more than a little nervous about the size of the investment. My dad's advice was that buying into property was always a good idea as people will always need houses. Yes, property can go up and down in value but that only matters if you're put in a position where you have to move when your house is worth less than you paid for it and particularly if it's worth less than what you owe on the mortgage (known as negative equity). Like pension investments, the value of housing generally increases more over the long term.

Research by property developer Stripe Property Group (see Lontayao 2022) has revealed how much a property in the UK cost 50 years ago and compared it with today's prices. When I was born, the average UK property was valued at £5,158. Adjusted for inflation, this still equates to an affordable £49,333 by today's standards. In 2022, the average UK homebuyer was paying £278,436 for the average property. That's a total increase of 464%, with house prices climbing by an average of 9.3%, or £4,582, every single year over the past 50 years. So it seems my dad's hunch was right – property is a good investment. It has some other advantages too, such as being exempt from inheritance tax if passed down to your direct family, and also gives you options to either downsize or take equity release in later life.

Rental is a secondary way to earn money from property

and is generally thought of as buying and renting out a separate property. It's less common but if you live in a house or large flat, why not think about renting out part of it to a lodger? This might sound slightly unnerving at first but having done it for more than ten years, we've found it to be safe, providing you take some common sense precautions in selecting your lodger and are clear on ground rules. It started when we were renovating our current house and Lou literally stumbled on one of her colleagues sleeping under a desk when she went into work early one morning. He'd been sleeping on his brother's sofa when a chip pan fire had gutted the flat and the insurance would only rehome the legal tenants. Our house was a bit of a building site but Lou offered him a mattress in the spare bedroom and before long he became an unofficial lodger, paying a nominal rent. A year or so later, when I was relocated for a stint of work up in Scotland, we decided to look for a formal lodger on a Monday to Friday basis so that Lou had the security of not living alone in a fairly rural area during the week.

We found that there's a good demand for such rentals, particularly among professionals who are working away from home on a contract but feel a hotel is too impersonal. There's also the advantage that they're not a permanent resident in your property; we always ensure that they have a registered family address elsewhere. A further benefit is a tax break (the 'rent a room' scheme), which allows you to earn up to a threshold of £7,500 per year tax free from letting out furnished accommodation in your home. When we started doing this, many friends said they couldn't possibly handle the intrusion of a lodger in their own home. Our view was that the lodger's rent and the additional tax benefit meant that they were paying our mortgage and contributed significantly to us being able to pay it off in our late forties. As with much of the advice in this book, it might not be for everyone but it demonstrates that you can achieve greater financial stability if you work hard at it and accept that sometimes you have to compromise.

On a similar theme, if you have a parking space, renting it out via one of the many available apps is also a great little earner, although sadly without any tax breaks. You might be lucky enough to live near a railway station or football stadium and that can give you a regular rental income.

The more common method of earning rental income is 'buy to let' (BTL) or buying another property to rent out. In general terms the concept here is twofold – earn a rental income that's higher than your mortgage and let the capital value of the house increase over time. BTL has been popular over the past 20 years, with some bold investors building large property portfolios. However, I'm not a complete convert. This comes down to the recurring theme of paying off your mortgage early or, to put it another way, are you borrowing to invest? This has led to a fundamental difference of opinion among financial commentators and many disagree with my view. If you borrow (on your mortgage) at 8% but your rental yield gives you 10%, you're 2% up. However, this only works in a steady state economy; if your mortgage goes up, you can't immediately increase your tenant's rent. And if you do have to remortgage, fees (often more than £1,000 for a good, market-leading rate) could wipe out that year's profit. If you're hit with a period without tenants (and it will happen, if only for a few months) you still have to pay the mortgage. You also need to factor in selling the properties at some point, and while their value is likely to have gone up, capital gains tax (CGT) will be due on any profit, and the allowances are much less generous than they used to be.

Lou and I haven't ignored BTL investments but we've gone about it in a slightly different way, which has provided a healthy property income. Twenty years ago, we bought an old farmhouse with a couple of acres and an attached 'granny annexe', as we wanted to futureproof an option to care for our parents. They were getting older and increasingly frail, plus they were living on the other side of the country. Prior to my in-laws moving in a few years ago, we rented it out but because it was technically part of the main property, it was included in our deeds and mortgage and not on a separate loan. We also had an old barn, which we were able to convert into a two-bed cottage. We strove not to increase the mortgage to build it (although being on an interest-only mortgage on the main house, we had some flexibility). In effect it has allowed us to have three rentals from one property – a lodger, plus the annexe and the cottage, both now mortgage free.

While this might sound idyllic, it's not been without some hardship. When we were looking for a property with an annexe and land, we had to accept that we'd have to compromise on location. We simply couldn't afford such a property near a large town or close to a motorway, so we're in quite a rural area on the edge of a small market town. We also had to buy somewhere that needed 'a bit of work', again down to cost, so we've spent a lot of time and effort on renovating the place. Being more rural has a knock-on impact on the availability of jobs and increased travel times but it was a conscious decision that worked out well in the end.

I appreciate that this won't be an option open to everyone, but it still supports the point of having rental income without the associated mortgage debt. We have rental income every month and the only outgoing is insurance and a bit of maintenance. This significantly reduces the risk to the rest of our finances and is why, when interest rates were increasing, it didn't affect us, allowing us to maintain rent at below market value. For us, happy, long-term tenants are preferable to pushing for a higher rent and potentially having a higher turnover of tenants.

Selling unwanted items

Consider selling your unwanted or unloved items. You've no doubt heard of eBay, where you take some photos, list an item for a low asking price and wait for the bids to flow in, with eBay taking a cut of the final sale price. There's a trade-off in starting with a low asking price to tempt buyers, the risk being that there will only be one person interested and they can buy it on the cheap. My preference is to look at similar items and price accordingly or list at a higher price, see if it's getting many hits and, if necessary, reduce the price. While I love eBay and have been a seller for many years, it requires a bit of effort and there are some new alternatives that I think are easier to use. One is Thrift, which was supported via an investment from the BBC's *Dragon's Den*. If you have a lot of clothes, particularly designer labels, and don't have much free time, this is a great option. You're sent a Freepost bag, which you fill with clothes and send off. Thrift sorts, photographs and lists the clothes, then you wait. When an item sells, Thrift takes a cut, a slice goes to charity and you get the rest in the form of a credit. I've used it on several occasions but have also bought clothes from the site. It's an efficient process and gives some money to charity, which is a bonus.

As I've mentioned previously, my current favourite site is Vinted. It's similar to eBay but I find it much easier to use. It's simple to upload photos and although the categorisation can be a little clunky, it's quick. The difference between eBay and Thrift is that with the latter the price you sell for is the price you get. With Vinted, the price you sell for is the price you get; the buyer pays the uplift for shipping, insurance and the site's margin, so it's clearer to see what you're earning. It also seems to be gaining traction as a popular selling platform, not least when things go wrong (such as a damaged parcel). Vinted takes care of it rather than you having to sort it out, as you would with eBay. The other advantage is that once listed, an item remains live until sold, so you don't have to keep relisting. Again, to avoid the risk of selling something too cheaply, you can always list at a higher price and then reduce it if it's not attracting much interest.

There are other local options such as Facebook Marketplace, Craigslist or Gumtree and you might have your own favourites but I find the ones I've mentioned above to be the least hassle. This flips back to the point about valuing your time accurately; if you list an item for £8 and it takes about an hour to photograph, list, relist, deal with seller communications, pack and you end up with £6.50 (less eBay commission) in the bank, you're earning less than the minimum wage. Amazon have an amusing acronym for similar situations where they just can't make a selling margin – CRAP: can't realise a profit. Sometimes you have to accept it's just not worth the effort.

Over the past year, we've listed and sold around 250 items and earned (or more accurately, 'recouped') about £2,000. It really is a random selection, from an umbrella, keyrings, hats, teaspoons and a ladder right through to a 1953 fly-fishing catalogue – anything that we no longer use or want and is relatively easy to ship; otherwise it's gifted to the charity shop. This 'easy to ship' point relates to the effort involved; like many others, we regularly shop on Amazon and they're kind enough to provide many boxes and packages, which I keep in our utility room. When I sell something, I recycle an Amazon box. My internal metric is that it shouldn't take me longer than five minutes to list, update, transact and ship an item, unless it's going for a reasonable price – then I might allow ten minutes!

I'll add two quick side notes on selling. First, if you're selling, 99% of the time you're going to get much (much) less than the retail price, so while it's nice to make £30 on a designer shirt, if you hadn't bought it in the first place for £80, you'd be £80 better off rather than £50 down. That said, we all tend to accumulate a lot of possessions and selling them on (or gifting them) is better than throwing them into landfill. The second point relates to our friends at the Inland Revenue (HMRC). My annual figure of about £2,000 is genuine but you need to be aware that there are tax laws regarding whether this is judged as income. If you're selling your own possessions (normally at a loss), you don't need to tell HMRC. There's one exception, though – if you sell something for more than £6,000 you might be liable for capital gains tax (excluding selling a car) but if you sell items you've made or have bought to sell on, and if you make more than £1,000 in sales, you might be deemed a trader and therefore have to declare it as additional income. Don't be tempted to ignore this, as HMRC does monitor these sites for evidence of trading.

Selling unwanted stuff is a good way to reduce clutter and gives someone else a chance to secure a bargain. If you have kids, it's a great way to teach them about the value of money. If they want a new toy, game or phone, sell some of their old items first and save for it. To ensure you're actually making some money and not just spending time selling things, it's a good idea to set up a separate bank account to channel sales into and also to use this money to buy related items for those sales, such as packing tape, labels, postage, etc. This way, you can see the balance build up and perhaps treat yourself to something once you've hit a certain target.

The gig economy

Whether you're in full or part-time employment, if you're in the right location some of the jobs in the gig economy are worth checking out – but they do tend to be more feasible in higher density residential areas. While at Amazon, I worked on the UK launch of Amazon Flex, which is designed to offer 'take it or leave it' blocks of work to delivery drivers. The concept behind this and similar platforms is great but there are some frustrations. To reduce management effort, there are some big algorithms sitting behind the technology, so if you have a problem, it's sometimes difficult to talk to a human and work it out, but overall the idea works. Many also use a surge pricing model, so during times of high demand such as Christmas, you can earn more than double for a 'block of work' – but you're also fighting against many others and it can be difficult to get accepted when it's convenient to you. Properly done, this new way of working is very flexible and without any commitments. I believe we'll see this type of work increase as technology expands into other markets, giving further options for earning extra income.

Cash savings

If you do have cash savings, make sure you have an account that pays reasonable interest. Many high street banks have a terrible reputation for not paying fair interest rates, so don't reward them with your loyalty – find a bank that does. Many offer attractive rates for a year then revert to a poor one, so unless you want to keep switching around for the best rate, pick one that's consistently near the top of the best buy tables and stick with it. As more financial institutions increase their security and multi-factor authentication, it's becoming more of an effort to keep switching and can also have an adverse effect on your credit rating. It's also worth sense-checking what the difference in rates means in real money terms. On an average balance of £5,000, 0.5% difference in interest is £25 – so ask yourself, is it worth it?

On a similar theme, many banks offer cashback if you switch your current account. This can be quite attractive, considering it's free money – up to £200 in some cases. The trick is to open a basic account, put a couple of direct debit payments through it and then use this 'donor account' to switch every year to another bank. Of the many hoops to jump through, there's normally a minimum amount to pay in. The banks don't seem to have clocked on to the fact that you can set up a standing order to transfer £1,000 each month (or whatever the minimum figure is) and then withdraw £900 the following day back into your main account, leaving a small balance for the direct debits.

Linked and affiliate spending

My last option to make some passive earnings is what I'd call linked or affiliate spending. Linked (or introductory) spending has taken over from what used to be cashback credit cards that gave you a percentage (in cash) against any spending. With more choice from online retailers and many more comparison websites, the cashback is paid if you shop through their site/portal. The reason they do this is to capture data about your spending habits (this is a growing trend often referred to as 'big data' – where technology now allows more complex analysis of larger data sets). Either way, they generally work well but there are a few golden rules to be aware of. There can be a long delay between a purchase and the cashback payment and the risk is that you lose track and don't claim – but if you select one and check it regularly, they can generate a reasonable return of a few hundred pounds with no real effort. As with any promotion, only use it for things you were going to buy anyway and never be tempted to buy something just on the basis of the cashback, as it's not guaranteed.

The final challenge is knowing whether or not you're actually getting a good deal. With the growing volume of data and more complex algorithms managing offers and pricing strategies, it can be confusing. I recently received an email from a seed catalogue with a link to an offer on some bedding plants, but since I knew they were in my preferred cashback site, I logged in through there, only to see a different price. Going direct to the retailer's website, I found yet another price! An even more complex challenge is when there are multiple layers. For example, through work I enrolled in the IHG loyalty scheme (Holiday Inn hotels group). I receive various benefits for being a 'loyal customer' (such as free nights) but I could also book a room at Holiday Inn through Hotels.com and receive a loyalty bonus from them as well. Finally, I could access Hotels.com via TopCashBack, which would give me cashback on my booking on top. Factoring this in against the variable pricing means you can tie yourself up in knots figuring out the best deal. It can become complicated to track the best price but it's worth looking at alternatives when you book online. My guidance would be to use one and stick with it but only for purchases you make regularly. Again, don't bank on it but you can get a nice bonus when the algorithms kick in and pay out. I booked some rooms for a summer break in Tenerife and hit a 'snap offer' of 11% cashback instead of the usual 1-2%. I was happy with the final price too, as I'd previously booked the same hotel for the same cost per night last year. Just to be clear, these are not recommendations, just my informal findings after using several of these sites. There are others, such as Quidco, Jam Doughnut or Airtime Rewards, to name a few – but the advice is the same as for a savings account. Don't chase them all, pick one you're comfortable with, don't overcomplicate it and, depending on your spending profile, you could end up with a nice bonus. Although we're now spending more on travel than others might, we have a pending cashback balance of £800 this year, which is worth having.

Loyalty and affinity cards

There's a crossover here with a section in Chapter 4 on saving money with loyalty cards. Depending on their structure, they can fit in both camps – creating savings and discounts on things you'd ordinarily buy, or earning rewards (that have financial value) that you can effectively bank. The credit card versions were originally 'cashback' cards, hence mentioning them in this chapter. They're becoming less common and the trend appears to be more software oriented or app based (such as the cashback sites mentioned above) where transactions are tracked in return for credits rather than being specifically tied to a single physical card. If you do have a credit card, it's definitely worth having one that gives you something back; just be sure that if it's a branded 'reward' you're able to convert it into a financial saving.

Tax tweaks

Finally, there are some tax tweaks you can use to make your earnings go further but this is a large and complex subject best dealt with by an independent financial advisor. It could include transferring some of your non-taxpaying spouse's allowance over to you to reduce your tax; entering a salary sacrifice scheme with your employer, where you reduce your salary (and therefore tax) in return for (typically) increased pension benefits; changing the beneficial ownership of jointly owned rental property; and not forgetting to use your annual ISA allowance for tax-free investments.

Side hustles

What exactly is a side hustle? There are several definitions of the word hustle, from a heightened state of activity or a sense of pace (as in 'hustle and bustle' or 'hustle along') but also slang interpretations suggesting an illicit activity or a swindle, both of which imply something quick, and possibly a bit dodgy. In the context of this book, I'm taking 'side hustle' to mean an easy, risk-free way to make additional money. My view is that this implies looking for a quick win in building wealth and I honestly don't believe there is such a thing. Yes, some people can and will make money out of the following ideas but I don't recommend them as I believe they have a high risk of not making much money, if any. While you could argue some of the subjects below are investments (and should be included in a later chapter), I'm including them here as I don't believe they're reliable enough for the regular person to have in their strategy. They do, however, often appear in media articles claiming to be a simple fast track to wealth – I find such posts tend to be a little light on the detail, usually focusing on a clickbait headline such as 'I made a million from XYZ in my spare time'. Similarly, every once in a while I see an article about investing in fine art, whisky or supercars quoting sensational returns but again, I wouldn't suggest these niche ideas for the average investor. In short, I don't believe there are such things as guaranteed short-term wins; investments should be over the long term and demonstrate a reliable growth trend.

Vlogs and influencing

There's an increasingly mature trend for influencers and online social media marketing. Despite what I've said previously, I don't totally disagree with marketing as a concept but I don't believe you should be persuaded to buy a product just because a well-known personality endorses it and I don't think there's long-term value in you becoming that 'personality' as a route to earning your fortune by posting about a particular product. Anyone can create an account and start posting content but there are now millions of people out there doing this and the odds of you earning a significant return for the time invested are low. Despite this, I'm interested in how people react to posts and am intrigued by what gets picked up by others. I love old architecture and also keep bees, these being the most common subjects of my Instagram posts. Maybe others don't find ancient architectural detail as interesting as I do but I get ten times as many likes and comments on almost any bee-related post. I'm all in favour of anyone posting about their passions but I don't see it as an income generator. Enjoy it for what it is rather than doing it in the hope that it will give you a financial return.

Cryptocurrency

This deserves a special mention; if you're tempted, do you understand what you're investing in or are you just following the crowd? I've no doubt that there might be a new form of currency in the future that's structured differently, particularly as physical cash is being used less often in favour of digital transactions. However, what that currency format will be, I don't know. I learned a little about cryptocurrency while mentoring a colleague over the course of a couple of years. He was much more technical than me and understood about the blockchain technology that sits behind crypto. He'd invested in a number of different cryptocurrencies and they were doing very well for him, valued at many times what he'd originally invested. I was sceptical about the stability of his returns and suggested he might want to sell some (at least his original stake) and then overall he wouldn't be out of pocket if it all fell apart. Rather than heed my advice, to my frustration he regularly invested more! He would try to explain his reasoning and the technical developments that were driving interest and therefore price but I never really understood it. This continued until he messaged me one day and said he needed to talk to me. He'd woken up in a cold sweat after dreaming it had all crashed and he'd lost everything. So, that morning, he sold his entire holding. He was exceptionally lucky, netting more than £300,000 in profits after paying a (large) CGT bill. A few months later, the value of cryptocurrencies fell through the floor, so his dream was a fortunate premonition.

As I write, the value of Bitcoin is still more than double what it was three years ago and others are nearly tenfold up on the same period but in my view, investing in crypto is still a huge gamble. Those who invested early may still make a reasonable return but as my grandfather used to say, 'If you see a bandwagon and try to jump on it, you're already too late.' I wasn't completely immune from the lure of huge gains but worked on the principle of only betting what I could afford to lose. I bought £1,000 in a handful of cryptocurrencies, took some profit when they increased in value but am 10% down overall and still have no real idea about how it all works.

It comes back to the fact that there will always be someone who has made a huge return but it's usually either down to luck, timing or a detailed knowledge of the product.

It's highly unlikely that the average person can replicate it, so I wouldn't recommend investing in something you don't understand.

Reselling returns and unsold stock

About ten years ago, we investigated buying from a trade wholesaler and selling some items online. The first thing we learned was that there was a minimum order of £1,000, which we weren't expecting but we decided to take a chance, buy some things we liked and see whether we could double our money within a year. The quick answer is yes, we did double our money, but we also learned a lot along the way. It was mainly about finding the right product to sell; we only sold out of half of the range we bought and were kicking ourselves for not buying more of it. The items that sold well were inconsistent; some items photographed well and looked 'worth the price' while others were heavy and awkward to ship and the cost of packaging and sending them wasn't really worth it. In the end we offloaded our remaining stock as a bulk buy on eBay. It was a worthwhile exercise but proved there's some luck involved in selecting something to sell and also effort in holding stock and managing the selling, not to mention time. Could we scale it up and do it instead of our main jobs? No, because although we enjoyed it and it was profitable, there was too much risk of ending up with dead stock, so we decided not to continue. Out of the 20 or so lines we bought, the best sellers (in terms of selling out and getting a good margin) were some ceramic and glass hurricane lights (none of which broke during shipping) and a fabric pig doorstop. Neither of us would have predicted these would be bestsellers.

A variation on this idea comes from the growth in online shopping and the associated increase in the number of items that are returned. For the retailer, processing these returns is expensive and they're often sold straight on to third party clearance houses, which auction them off. You can buy these pallets as a bit of a lucky dip of stock to sell on and you can find some real gems in there but there's no guarantee you'll hit the jackpot. Unfortunately, the media only spins the one pallet that turns a huge profit rather than the many that don't.

Returned and refurbished items are classed A, B or C, with 'Grade C' being the most common. Definitions vary, but might typically be: 'Inventory has been inspected, tested and restored to the original manufacturer's operating specifications. This fully functioning product is in retail-ready condition but with significant cosmetic defects (significant blemishes and/or significant scratches, dents or frame damage)'. In other words, it works, but may not look great. There's usually also a disclaimer that says the inventory list might not be accurate and you buy at your own risk. Looking at a sample lot, one pallet of kitchen/electrical returns had 169 items ranging from a Black & Decker vacuum cleaner and DeLonghi coffee machine down to a photo frame, an ice-cream scoop and an egg timer. The retail value was £3,026 and the pallet was being offered at 18% of this or £544 plus delivery (£45), unless you went to collect it. There's a rule of thumb when reselling most surplus stock that 10% (of the retail price) is good value – but that's if you can find a buyer. It's all down to risk; you could be lucky and get a pallet full of high-end branded items that you can sell at an attractive margin but a lot of it will be mid-range stock and cosmetically imperfect. For the reasons above, I see it as just too high risk and it also consumes too much time and space to recommend as a good money-making idea. If you have a passion for a product and find a good supply, I'm all for doing a little buying and selling – but it's not for everyone.

Drop-shipping

If the risk associated with buying and selling is the physical stock holding (either in terms of space or being left with unsold items), then it follows that if you remove this risk, it might be more viable. Enter drop-shipping. I first came across this in a distribution company where we built a drop-ship agreement with a tool supplier. They traditionally sold their tools directly in shops and via a physical catalogue. We wanted to sell their tools but didn't want to hold stock in our warehouse, so we listed their tools in our catalogue and when we made a sale, we sent an electronic order to them to ship to our customer but with paperwork quoting us as the retailer. We received a trade discount and the customer was none the wiser; the tool manufacturer received wider exposure for their products, we could offer our customers a bigger range and we made a small profit. It was win–win – more sales and very little effort.

This was in the pre-internet age, with only basic electronic messaging possible between systems, but technology has completely changed this landscape. You're now able to set yourself up as a drop-shipper (Shopify is an established and popular choice for your sales platform), effectively listing products that someone else is selling. When someone buys from you, it triggers your purchase of the item but ships it to your customer. A difference against the traditional model is that you don't need to have a contract with the 'supplier' and in many cases they may be completely unaware. Although you can build a business like this, and many have, I do have some reservations about the long-term viability of this new model. For example, you want to start selling shirts. You create your account and use the technology to find a range of shirts, set your price and list them. I've just searched for 'purple shirt' on Amazon and it's returned 148 results

– an extremely wide range for an unusual item. Consider whether a number of drop-shippers are now also listing the same items on their platforms. The physical range of shirts on offer stays the same but the (virtual) range of shirts on offer to the customer increases, all with small variations in price. Therefore I don't believe this is a great experience for the customer!

Despite my reservations, it's an emerging use of technology and I predict it will continue in some form – but I don't see it meeting my criteria for long-term proven returns just yet. Yes, you can curate a range of products and sell through this channel but the margins are low and it does carry some risk.

Matched betting

Technology has also opened up a whole new world of potential quick wins that in theory can generate significant returns but, as is often said, 'If it sounds too good to be true, it probably is.' The sheer pace at which technology allows someone to develop an app or a platform means that it can be a while before companies close whichever loophole you might be taking advantage of. A good example is a concept known as 'matched betting.' Online betting is a growing trend and bookmakers are chasing market share, often offering free bets after you've created an initial account and placed your first bet. Just searching for 'free bets' returned a number of offers: 'Stake £10 and get £40 in free bets.' The concept is simple; place two bets on a game between two players, each bet against one of the players winning. Obviously, one will win, and one will lose. You might not win much, but you won't have lost, and you've 'earned' your free bets. You register twice, get two free bets and bet again on both players winning. One of them does and you've made a profit as you didn't pay any stake money for the bet. I feel this is a little disingenuous and not in the spirit of betting on the outcome of a sporting match, so it's not something I support despite the technical approach of generating free money. I also think such schemes will be closed down by regulators as they wise up to them but will be replaced by another equally cunning approach in a different industry. It doesn't seem honest and isn't something I'd suggest as a viable long-term strategy for your finances.

Summary

As a route to creating wealth, your primary lever is your career, followed closely by your pension. An option for many is leveraging a property, then a number of smaller approaches can yield a few thousand in additional earnings per year. Together with spending less, if you invest these savings into either your mortgage or pension, you're on the way to improving your financial position. There are other ways to make some money 'on the side' but all involve a little effort and risk. I'm not saying don't look at them but don't bank on them being a core part of your strategy as there are no shortcuts to real wealth creation.

Key takeaways

→ Proactively manage your career and aim to make incremental steps, ultimately increasing your base salary.

→ Pensions have two big wealth-creating levers: free money from either tax breaks or employer contributions (or both) and being invested over a long period of time.

→ Your own property can be wealth creating but be mindful of the cost of servicing that investment (your mortgage).

→ Declutter and sell things you no longer need or want.

→ Select one or two purely passive loyalty schemes and don't try to chase every offer going.

→ Whatever you do to earn more, think about the time and effort it consumes to evaluate what's the best value; aim for zero time (totally passive) or big benefit (pensions) and ignore ideas that take too much effort with too little reward.

→ Be wary of schemes that sound too good to be true – they probably are.

How does the
stock market
work?

Chapter 6

Investment basics

This chapter is going to cover the meaty topic of investments
– but don't worry, it's not going to be overcomplicated
or maths heavy. It's intended to show you the range of
investment types out there, how they work, their pros and
cons, and help you decide what might be suitable for you.
I'll reiterate that I'm not a professional financial advisor and
these are only my opinions based on the approach we've
taken to our investments.

I've also had years of experience of being a workplace
pension trustee, tracking my own investments and talking
to financial providers, quizzing them on how their products
work. And I've talked to many friends and colleagues, who
have often said they've had some financial advice but didn't
really understand what it meant. As mentioned previously,
I support seeking independent financial advice, but since
you generally have to pay for it, I'd like to think this overview
of personal finance will help you ask the right questions for
your situation and also help you to better understand the
answer (options or proposals). I want you to feel you've
had value for money and information that's useful to you.
I'll share some of the investment decisions we've made
but it's by no means a recommendation to follow them

– it's purely to illustrate how we have created our own investment strategy.

Pensions

As previously mentioned, pensions are a great long-term investment, not least because of the tax advantages but equally because you can't dip into them if tempted. Private pensions are either personal or company based. Company, workplace or occupational pensions are also split into two – defined benefit (DB) or defined contribution (DC). Defined benefit pensions are generally older schemes or from public sector employment such as the police, NHS or civil service. They're based on the concept of a long career within the service and when you retire you receive a defined benefit or guaranteed pension payment, normally a percentage of your final salary in the job (hence these are often referred to as final salary schemes). These schemes are great if you have one but a headache to the organisation providing it, which is why they're less common nowadays outside the public sector.

It's all down to risk and certainty of investment performance. These schemes take in variable contributions from employees but guarantee that a specific pension value will be paid out – and given that investment returns are never guaranteed (values can go down as well as up), would you take that risk? I know I wouldn't! Funding these schemes is expensive, which is why the employer contribution in public sector jobs is high – because it needs to be. If you do have a DB pension accumulated over many years, it's worth keeping and planning your career accordingly, as it could provide a significant boost to your final pension.

The DC pension is much more common. In this type of scheme, contributions (inputs) are defined rather than the benefits (payouts). In a company pension, both you and your employer contribute (including your own company, if you're self-employed), whereas for a personal pension, it's just you making contributions. The personal pension is also referred to as a self-invested personal pension (SIPP). Changes in legislation in 2015 allowed you to start drawing from your SIPP at 55 (rising to 57 in 2028), while DB schemes will specify a retirement date (more likely nearer state retirement age)

Whichever type of pension you have, you put money in, it's invested over time with the intention of growing in value and then it provides an amount (your pension pot) that you can withdraw as a pension. This is in addition to the State Pension, which we'll cover shortly. You might also find that you end up with several different pension pots as you move jobs because each company scheme manages investments slightly differently. It can be a challenge to keep track of them, particularly if you move house as well as jobs. Company pensions are now tightly regulated and generally well run. However, having several smaller investment pots can attract multiple management charges and they may also be investing in duplicate or conflicting funds. Therefore, if you do have several pensions, it's worth tracking them down and consolidating them into your own SIPP. Many SIPP providers offer help with tracking down old pensions, so even if you've lost the paperwork, it's not that difficult. Company pensions invest in a set number of funds with little choice for you as an investor, whereas in a SIPP you need to make that investment selection yourself – but you don't need to be a financial wizard to make a sound investment choice. I believe it's better to have one single pension scheme by the time you reach retirement as there are a couple of alternatives for how you take out your money and it's easier to manage one pot.

Traditionally, when you retired, you'd look at your pension pot and take out an annuity, which is a financial product bought for a fixed price (your total pension value) that pays you your pension. There are different ways to get that pension paid and since it's a commercial product, you can get quotes from different providers. By way of an example, if you had a pension pot of £200k at age 60, you could (at current rates) be paid a guaranteed pension of £8,725 a year for the rest of your life. Alternatively, you could be paid £17,175 a year for ten years and then take a £20k final lump sum (by which time you'd be receiving your State Pension), or you could take it all as a cash lump sum, which would be a total payment of £139,154 (after paying £60,846 in tax). There are many more alternative payment variations and this final taxation also comes with options; you're entitled to receive 25% of your pension tax free (the rest is taxed as income) but you can either take it as a lump sum at the start of your pension or incrementally as you take monthly pension payments.

This is a complex area and subject to changing tax legislation but the trend is moving away from annuities (because they're not paying out as much as they used to) and moving towards a flexible drawdown. I won't go into detail about how to choose the most efficient way to be paid your pension but it's worth understanding the variables, not least because knowing how you spend your money and what you spend it on will help you formulate a plan for how best to draw your pension. When you reach this stage, it's definitely worth seeking independent advice, but to get the best value from that, you need to have an idea about what your retirement expenditure might be.

One of the most difficult financial exercises we had to do was about five years ago when we did some cash flow modelling with an advisor to sense-check whether we really could afford to stop working. It was all very well having a vague plan of 'more travel, new car, downsizing the house' but it took time to develop a strong idea of what that retirement spending might look like and in particular the timing of changes such as downsizing. For some, retirement holidays might include a cruise and skiing every year, while for others it might be exploring Europe in a motorhome. Similarly, it might be treating yourself to a Range Rover or a Porsche, or going from two cars down to one. Everyone's plan will be different but the basics of building that plan are the same.

If you were born after 1978, you'll be entitled to a State Pension from the age of 68 (although this may change). A full State Pension is currently worth approximately £205 a week or just over £10k a year. However, it depends on you having made National Insurance (NI) contributions throughout your employment. If your NI contributions fall short in some years, you may receive less. If you do one thing after reading this book, it should be to go online and check your current State Pension forecast (www.gov.uk/check-state-pension). It will estimate your pension and flag up any years you're missing NI contributions. You may be able to 'buy back' those missing years and increase your eventual payment. This is invariably worthwhile as the State Pension is (currently) protected by a 'triple lock' agreement whereby it increases each year by the average increase in earnings, inflation or 2.5% – whichever is higher. In 2023, there was a generous increase of 10% due to inflation being high, so it's worth filling in any gaps. I predict this arrangement will change as funding the State Pension is a huge burden on the government but I believe there will always be an intent to keep it in line with cost of living increases.

To sum up, pensions can be complicated but don't ignore them – they're a valuable tool in your kitbag to help you shape a financially stable future. It's worth noting that there are several safeguards when it comes to pension investments.

Company and occupational schemes are usually protected by the Pension Protection Fund and SIPP investments are protected by the Financial Services Compensation Scheme (up to certain limits).

ISAs and other tax-free investments

Individual savings accounts or ISAs are second to pensions in terms of tax-beneficial investments. Again, these are subject to change but I'd expect there to be some element of tax efficiency with any new scheme. Whereas pensions are effectively tax free to contribute to (but money taken out is taxed), ISAs are the reverse – you invest your (taxed) income but when you withdraw money, any gains are totally tax free. There's an annual investment limit (in 2024, £20k a year) and you can withdraw money at any time but you can't reinvest beyond £20k in any given tax year. You can save into a cash ISA but these are generally on par with the best savings accounts so aren't that attractive. You can also invest in a stocks and shares ISA and select the same types of funds as you have in your pension.

There are also two further variations on the ISA theme. A lifetime individual savings account (LISA) can be used to help save for a home, retirement or both (the government provides a bonus of up to £1,000 per year until you reach the age of 50); and a junior ISA (JISA) is a long-term savings plan that can be opened by a parent or legal guardian to invest in a child's future, allowing them to receive a tax-free lump sum once they've turned 18. Successive governments may change any of these schemes and their limits or allowances. Although you could view an ISA as just another savings account, don't discount its potential as a highly effective, tax-free option. HMRC figures suggest that there were more than 4,000 ISA millionaires in 2021 – in other words, investors who have contributed to their ISAs each year and now have a total investment value of more than £1 million. This number has grown significantly year on year and is nine times more than in 2016.

The three-way investment choice

For many years, we've taken a spring holiday in the Canary Islands and always set aside a few hours in the sunshine to chat over how we'd invest any 'spare' money before the end of the tax year. The three-way choice was usually:

1. pay some more off our mortgage to reduce the overall interest
2. make some additional pension contributions, get the tax benefit and let it grow over the long term
3. use up our ISA allowance for the year in the knowledge that any gains would be tax free.

There's no right answer here and over the years we've picked them all, or more often split any money we have between all three on the basis that doing something was better than doing nothing.

Once you've chosen your investment vehicle, there are four core elements you can invest in (shares, managed funds, trackers or bonds), which I'll outline below and highlight some of the benefits and costs of each. They apply equally to pensions and ISAs, the difference being the limits of what you can put in, when you can take them out and how they're taxed.

Shares, stocks or equities

These represent small portions (shareholdings) of an individual company. Take, for example, the drinks company Diageo. Ownership is split into approximately 2.56 million shares and at the time of writing each one was worth around £3.26. You can buy any number of shares in your pension or ISA. There's a small difference in the buying and selling price of the share to cover trading costs but you're free to buy any publicly traded share in the UK or overseas. Shares are traded on the stock market, which goes up or down in value depending on trading conditions, press releases or the company's general health and outlook. You buy shares in the belief that the company is well run and growing and therefore the share price will rise, or that the company will pay a dividend to shareholders. In essence, dividends are the excess profit the company has made in a year and they're usually paid back to shareholders, expressed as a percentage of the share price. It's referred to as the 'dividend yield' and as I write, Diageo sits at 2.45%.

Buying shares can be a profitable endeavour but it's a risky business as you're betting on a single company and there are many unforeseen factors that can challenge it, however big or established the organisation. There's also the question of timing the sale of the shares, as that's when you get your money back. You either pick a share that's increasing in value and ensure that you sell before it drops off, or you invest in a company that has a reliable dividend yield. Ideally, you want both but there are fewer unicorns around and if you do see one, it's not likely to remain favourable in the long term. Individual shares aren't really suitable for the novice investor. However, many platforms allow you to build a virtual portfolio of shares and track how your stock picking would have fared. Unless you're confident with your investments, leave individual shares to others and don't be tempted by 'hot tips' from any number of sources just because you've read that a particular company is undervalued and set to double in size over the next year. I've held a fair number of shares over the years but there have been just as many that have gone nowhere as those that have done spectacularly well (my Tesla holding increased tenfold). So, while I consider myself to be a successful investor by virtue of my current financial position, I'm no expert. What I've learned is to spread the risk.

Funds

Rather than taking a punt on an individual company, a safer alternative is to invest in a fund or selection of shares selected along a theme and looked after by an investment manager. Funds can be geographical (Asia, Japan), focused on performance (high dividend yields or growth) or the size or type of business (small companies or pharmaceuticals, for example). They all have a particular niche and each fund manager believes their selection is the best. As you can guess, they can't all be right and there's no such thing as the perfect fund, leading to a very wide range to choose from. There are some well-known fund managers such as Warren Buffett (Berkshire Hathaway) and Terry Smith (Fundsmith Equity) but success is never guaranteed, as proven by Neil Woodford's fund collapsing in 2019. Buffett and Smith follow a similar mantra of buying shares in good quality companies at a fair price and then keeping them over an extended period of time. The intricacies of what constitutes a good quality company are detailed and subjective but include how resilient it has been over time, barriers to competition and consistent growth or dividends. Warren Buffett is also known as the 'Sage of Omaha' and is often quoted for his insight into how he has successfully invested over the years. You'll find several of them, or versions of them, throughout this book, such as 'Never invest in a company you don't understand' and 'It's far better to buy a wonderful company at a fair price than a fair company at a wonderful price.'

Like shares, funds pay a dividend, which behave like individual share dividends. But unlike shares (where you pay a fee for buying and then selling), with a fund you pay a percentage management charge. This covers the cost of the management team who are looking after the investment decisions. Over my investing history, I've moved away from managed funds in favour of trackers but where I do have some, I still look at the fees in relation to their long-term performance and don't think anything over 1% is good value (as an example, I hold some in Fundsmith Equity, which I mentioned earlier). Alongside fees and yield, there's the physical growth of the fund, which again varies. Looking at Figure 7, you can see two funds with yields of around 6%, with 1% variance in fees. But their overall performance has differed: the table shows annual performance (fund growth) over the past five years (noting nearly all funds were impacted by Covid-19), with the final column showing the cumulative five-year growth. The third fund in this table has no yield quoted; it's called an accumulation fund, where the dividend is reinvested (noting the higher cumulative growth). Funds where the dividend is paid out are called income funds. As you can see in Figure 7, performance is variable, making fund selection a challenge; popular platform Hargreaves Lansdown offers nearly 4,000 to choose from. Depending on their strategy, fund managers will buy and sell investments within their fund with the aim of improving their overall performance.

Fund	Yield	Fees	2018/19	2019/20	2020/21	2021/22	2022/23	5 Year
Jupiter Monthly Alternative Income	6.79%	1.70%	3.66%	-3.67%|	18.74%	-4.76%	-13.17%	-1.95%
Legal & General Strategic Bond Fund	6.10%	0.63%	5.21%	7.01%	9.67%	-9.77%	5.51%	17.47%
Barings Global Dividend	0.00%	0.86%	11.45%	3.97%	7.64%	-2.08%	8.96%	33.08%
Fundsmith Equity	1.09%	0.94%	11.58%	15.88%	17.40%	-12.14%	13.72%	51.66%

Figure 7: Performance of a selection of managed funds. Source: Hargreaves Lansdown

There's a further variation on managed funds that I'll use in an example later on and those are hedge funds. These are higher risk and use a number of different investment strategies beyond just buying and selling shares. They can produce high returns but this higher risk means they're mainly for wealthy investors with a minimum investment of high net worth.

Tracker funds

If funds are less risky than individual shares but cost more to invest in, is there a middle ground? Enter automated tracker funds. Every share sits in a market or index – for example, the Financial Times Stock Exchange (FTSE), which has an index of the top 100 UK shares (FTSE 100); or Standard and Poor's (S&P 500), which lists the top 500 shares on all US markets. Automated tracker funds seek to replicate the market or index and therefore have low costs as they involve little human intervention (known as passive investing) and ongoing costs are fractions of a per cent against an actively managed fund, which could be 0.5–1.5%. As a general rule, the world's economies are growing and therefore nearly all markets have increased in value, particularly when looked at over the long term. And although a tracker fund can never truly match the index (since it's following or copying end of day positions), they track sufficiently closely, particularly the larger funds. Provided you're investing for the long term, you can take advantage of low cost and growth with a tracker.

In 2008, Warren Buffett issued a challenge to the hedge fund industry, which in his view charged exorbitant fees that the funds' performances couldn't justify. One such hedge fund (Protégé Partners) took on the million-dollar bet and lost. Buffett's contention was that, including fees, costs and expenses, an S&P 500 index fund would outperform a hand-picked portfolio of hedge funds over ten years. While there's a place for active fund management, there's also a compelling case for passive tracker investing. It's one that I've been drawn to over the years and now forms a significant part of our portfolio. They're also easy to understand and don't require a huge amount of knowledge to be able to select the suitable tracker, and we'll use the S&P 500 as an example in later chapters.

To demonstrate this, compare the data in the Figure 8 for two trackers against the managed funds in Figure 7. Simply put, they cost less but deliver more. That's why I like them.

Fund	Yield	Fees	2018/19	2019/20	2020/21	2021/22	2022/23	5 Year
UBS S&P 500 Index	1.23%	0.09%	6.09%	11.93%|	25.77%	2.62%	9.98%	68.57%
Fidelity Index World	1.61%	0.12%	4.69%	7.67%	23.41%	-2.51%	12.53%	52.60%

Figure 8: Performance of two index tracker funds. Source: Hargreaves Lansdown

There's a variant called an exchange traded fund (EFT) that's common in tracking an index and it works essentially the same as a regular fund except the way they're structured normally means they're a little cheaper, so many of my tracker investments are more correctly EFTs.

Gilts or bonds

These are effectively IOUs from governments or large institutions and used to borrow money. UK government bonds are known as gilts because, historically, the paper certificates issued had a gold edge; in the US, they're called treasuries. On the basis that governments aren't meant to go bankrupt, their yield is more stable than shares, whose price can be volatile. Here we come back to risk and the volatility of shares; it's generally accepted that while share prices can be volatile, they can also produce a higher return, particularly when viewed against more stable gilts. Again, a common approach is that, early in your investment timeline, you're encouraged to invest in equities (shares) as the overall gains smooth out any short-term losses. As you near retirement, many managed pensions will start switching from equities to gilts so that the risk of a short-term loss is reduced. The last thing you want the year before drawing your pension is for the value to drop by 10%, so in theory it's not a bad strategy.

As we know, nothing is guaranteed and surprises can appear from anywhere. The astonishing events that unfolded after Boris Johnson left office in 2023 and Liz Truss and Kwasi Kwarteng announced their disastrous budget was a case in point. Economists weren't convinced that the £45 billion of unfunded tax cuts would drive economic growth and pay for itself in the way the government believed. With inflation at a 40-year high, a rising risk of recession and higher borrowing costs, it was a big gamble at the wrong moment. International financial reaction was swift and damning. The pound fell to its lowest-ever level against the dollar, while gilt prices collapsed. Off the back of a very tentative recovery from Covid-19, this completely trashed the markets and unexpectedly shattered the value of all those 'safe' investments.

While a market collapse is clearly a crisis for those actively accessing their pension funds, for many of us, what goes down eventually comes back up and by the time you retire, this blip could well be forgotten. I say 'could' and want to unpick this a little more and demonstrate that for the average person, when it comes to investing, simple is best and you should be wary of many 'financial experts'. Way back in 1990 when he was chancellor, Gordon Brown removed the option for pension funds to receive dividends free of tax. No regular voter on the street really noticed (nor cared); it generated huge sums for the Treasury but cost pension funds billions over the following years. But it wasn't all bad news, because under the Labour government, companies were forced to declare the financial health of their pension funds, with many reporting that they couldn't meet their liabilities (in other words, they didn't have sufficient investments to pay out their employees' guaranteed pensions). Around this time, British Telecom held the UK's second-biggest pension fund and it was almost £8 billion in the red. In part, this led to the demise of the DB pension as BT couldn't fund it themselves. To get round this problem, financial experts created an investment vehicle called a liability-driven investment or LDI. Without going into detail, these are leveraged tools to borrow against the assets within a pension fund. Notwithstanding that many pension assets are 'safe' bonds and the fact that the value of UK pension funds is somewhere in the region of £3 trillion, you start to see why the financial markets went into meltdown as bond prices collapsed.

I'm not going to side with one political party or another as in my view both have pursued flawed policies in their time. If

I'm going to attribute any blame, it's to the large financial institutions that are gambling with ever more complex financial tools in order to create a return. So when you're at the stage where you're reading an investment report or getting financial advice and someone suggests they have an investment that is 'specially structured' to generate impressive returns, I'd be extremely sceptical. I like to understand what I'm investing in and therefore prefer simple concepts.

The above section covers the core investment types and these will form the basis of your investment portfolio. Given the lack of guaranteed returns and other complexities, our own investment approach has been governed by simplicity, alongside investing for the long term. For the vast majority, investing in a basic tracker fund is going to be a sound decision. There are still choices to make in terms of which tracker or index to track but it's a good baseline to start from.

Now we'll delve into the mechanics of investing, some of which might seem minor but can have a huge influence on the returns you can achieve.

Reinvesting dividends and compound interest

Dividends can be viewed in the same way as interest on a savings account. You get an annual percentage return on whatever value you've invested. More important potentially than the actual percentage rate is what Einstein allegedly referred to as 'the eighth wonder of the world' – compound interest. In essence, it's interest on interest and it has an astonishing effect over the long term.

Consider this scenario: you invested £10,000 in your ISA at age 20 and picked an index tracker that returned 4%. In the first year, you'd have an additional £400 (£10,400 in total). Assuming the same return the following year, you'd get 4%

of £10,400, giving you an additional £16 on the £400 interest figure from the previous year, resulting in a total of £10,816. In 10 years, it would have grown to £14,802 and in 20 years, £21,911, more than double the original £10,000 invested, all from 4%. Let's consider the FTSE 100, which has on average returned 12% over each of the past ten years. Plugging this into the above example, £10,000 invested would have grown to just over £33,000, less any platform and fund fees. This underlines the value of starting your investments, however small, as early as possible.

It's worth taking a moment here to reflect on the interest element of your repayment mortgage discussed earlier. Paying interest on a loan follows similar maths to the interest paid on your savings but in reverse. If you buy into the idea of compound interest generating you a good return on savings, then I hope it explains why I prioritised reducing the mortgage balance and therefore interest paid to the bank.

Inflation

This refers to the general rise in the price of goods such that the purchasing power of the pound in your pocket buys less than it used to and is linked to the retail price index (the average change month on month in the price of goods and services purchased by most households in the UK). If the rate of inflation is higher than your investment returns then, overall, you've not made any progress. Although inflation hit a record high of 11.1% in October 2022, the rolling average over the past ten years is less than 3%, so while there's short-term pain in your household budget, longer-term investments should be able to perform against inflation.

There's an interesting argument relating to the value of debt in times of high inflation. Just as the buying power of your cash is eroded over time, if you maintain a debt (such as a mortgage) over the same period, the value of that debt may still be £100k but after inflation is taken into account in real terms it's equivalent to a lower value. However, this is a little theoretical and I still subscribe to the approach of paying off your mortgage debt as quickly as possible, not least because it de-risks you from any further interest changes or remortgaging costs.

Pound cost averaging

This is an odd-sounding concept that essentially means it's better to drip-feed an investment with smaller, regular amounts than a single lump sum. The calculations are a little messy but it's easier to visualise graphically (see Figure 9). Take, for example, a share that's valued at £10 in January. You buy 1,200, for an investment of £12,000. Over the next year, the share price varies between £13.25 and £7.50. Consider if you'd instead have invested £1,000 every month. The average share price over the 10 months is still £10 but buying in smaller, monthly investments has allowed you to buy 1,227 shares for your investment of £12,000, at an average share price of £9.78, or a discount of £0.22 per share.

Granted, if there were dividends due in the period, the first option would have yielded a higher dividend payout but the advantage of pound cost averaging is that it's considerably easier to invest a smaller amount regularly than a lump sum and therefore the ability to buy more when the share price is lower contributes to outweighing a single lump sum investment. It also reduces the risk that you invest your lump sum at a high point in the market which then drops. We'd all like to buy at the lowest price but don't know when that might be, so spreading the investment reduces the risk of inadvertently investing all your money at the top of the market.

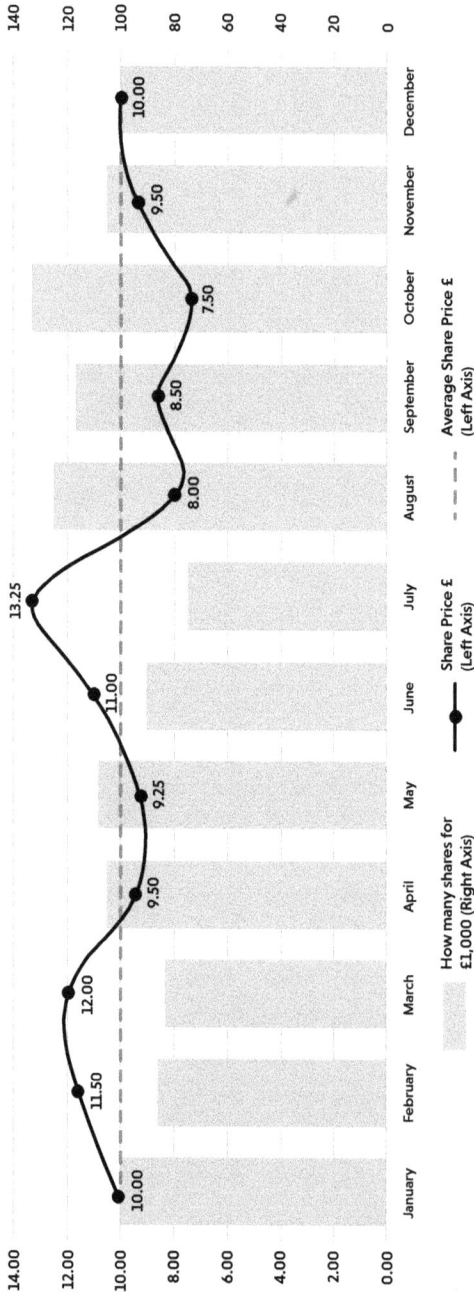

Figure 9: Example of pound cost averaging: the advantages of regular investing over a single lump sum

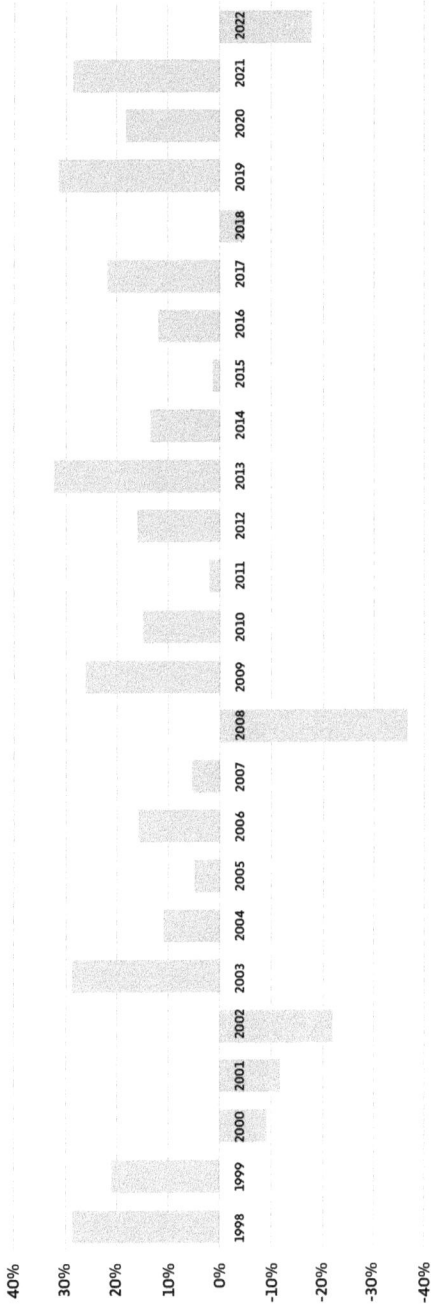

S&P500 Annual % Return (including Dividends) 1998-2022

Figure 10: S&P 500 annual percentage return 1998 to 2022

S&P Average Closing Price (1995-2022)

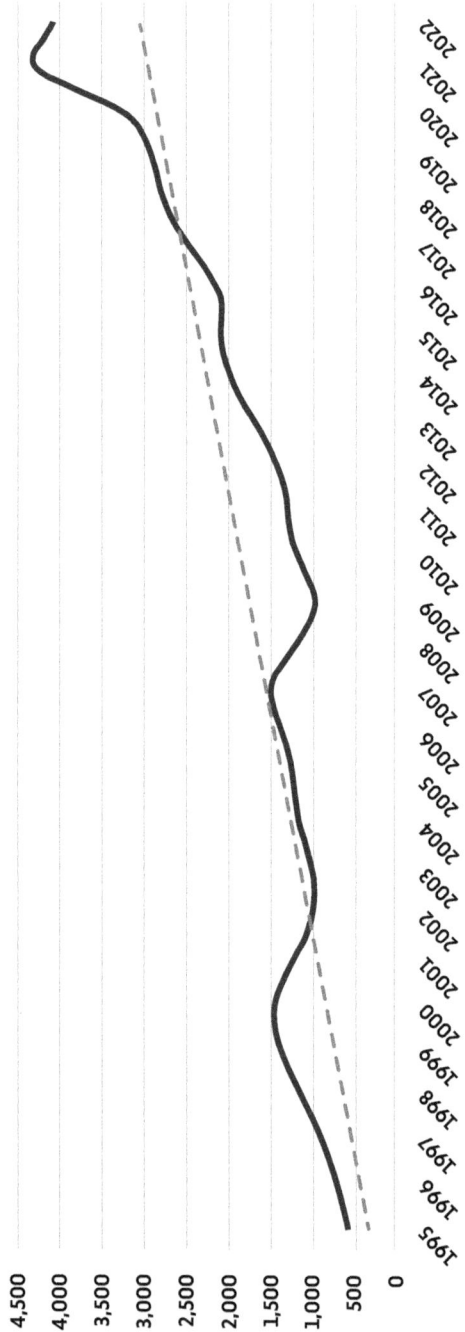

Figure 11: S&P 500 average closing price 1995 to 2022

Performance

Let's take the S&P 500 as an example and look at overall growth and annual returns (see Figure 10, previous page). The S&P 500 is a benchmark of US stock performance and since its creation in 1957 it has returned an annual average of more than 11% through to 2021. Figure 10 shows those returns over the past 25 years, with only six years failing to make a positive return. Other than more often making a return than a loss, there's no particular trend and this is where it's advantageous to use pound cost averaging over an extended period to smooth performance and generate a reliable return rather than trying to pick a winning investment on any given day.

Given this trend in returns, it's no surprise that, overall, the market has grown in tandem from an average closing price in 1995 of 541 to 4,097 in 2022. In other words, the combined financial size of those 500 US companies has grown dramatically over the past 27 years.

In the developed world, most economies and therefore stock market indices are growing over time. Clearly there are challenging times when economies shrink, either through political instability or a global shock such as Covid-19, but in the long term the trend is up. Although it's not particularly ground breaking, this is key to my investment philosophy: I invest little and often over the long term. You don't need to pay extra fees for someone to try to beat the market; just ride the market itself for a much lower cost. Compound interest shows the power of reinvesting returns but the real leverage comes when it's applied over a longer period.

I'll add one final comment – and again, it stems from a Warren Buffett quote, 'Be fearful when others are greedy and greedy when others are fearful.' When a stock is popular (or when there's high demand and buyers are greedy for it) the stock price rises; however, the value of what you're buying has reduced as you're paying more for the same number of shares. When a stock is out of favour in the market and there's less demand, the price falls. Providing the underlying business is still solid, you can pay a lower price for it and get better value.

The reason I highlight this is to reinforce the fact that even though shares, indices or a market can drop in value, it's not always something to worry about. If anything, provided you believe in the underlying growth proposition of that company or economy over the long term, then you're buying in at a lower price and getting better value for money, as in the pound cost averaging example. So while I'm not too concerned about a drop in the market and see it as a potential buying opportunity, beware of any company whose share price is falling because they are themselves failing. Every so often a business will fail, possibly because it hasn't kept up with market trends or technology and the share price falls, making it look like a potential bargain against the previous year's results. But if it's a dead duck, it's not good value. Examples include HMV and Kodak, companies that completely failed to keep pace with technology. At its height in 1994, Kodak was worth $20 billion but it ignored the potential of digital cameras (despite inventing them) and sales fell off a cliff from $14 billion to $2 billion, with the company falling into bankruptcy in 2012. Cheap doesn't always mean good value.

The time to be more concerned about a market dip is if you have to sell, or liquidate, your investments and end up selling at a potential loss – but there are strategies to manage that as you reach retirement. However, if you're an investor in your thirties and not looking to retire for the next 30 years or so, I'd advise you to ride it out and it will bounce back. It probably won't be a surprise that I look at my investments on a daily basis and, yes, I get a little grumpy if I see they have gone down – but I don't panic, as I've learned over the past decade or so that what goes down does come up again and when that happens, I'm happy!

To prove that this isn't all theoretical, I'm sharing an extract from my personal tracker from pre-Covid-19 days, over two years. The investment value includes our pensions and ISAs. There are some caveats to this graph (Figure 12, overleaf) in that I was still employed during 2020 and contributing to my pension, though we were incrementally adding to ISAs and had started drawing down from Lou's pension in 2021, so it's not as pure a picture as the S&P 500 example but it shows similar trends. Yes, it was a shock to see more than £100k wiped off at the start of Covid-19 but it has recovered well and I believe it still has a way to go.

Duplication

When I started working and enrolled in my first company pension, I received a piece of advice that sparked my investment journey. There used to be a second part to the State Pension that was known as the State Earnings Related Pension Scheme (SERPS) but you could opt out of it and invest the money elsewhere. I wouldn't have done this but two of my school friends were taking a gap year while working for Norwich Union (now Aviva) and the company suggested this to them. If you opted out, you needed a private pension to pay the SERPS money into and I arrogantly thought that I might be better off managing my own money than leaving it to the government, so I gave it a go. This started off my personal pension (now SIPP) and the opportunity to pick investments. I was like a kid in a sweet shop; I jumped at almost every tip I read and invested in all sorts of oddball funds and shares. However, over time,

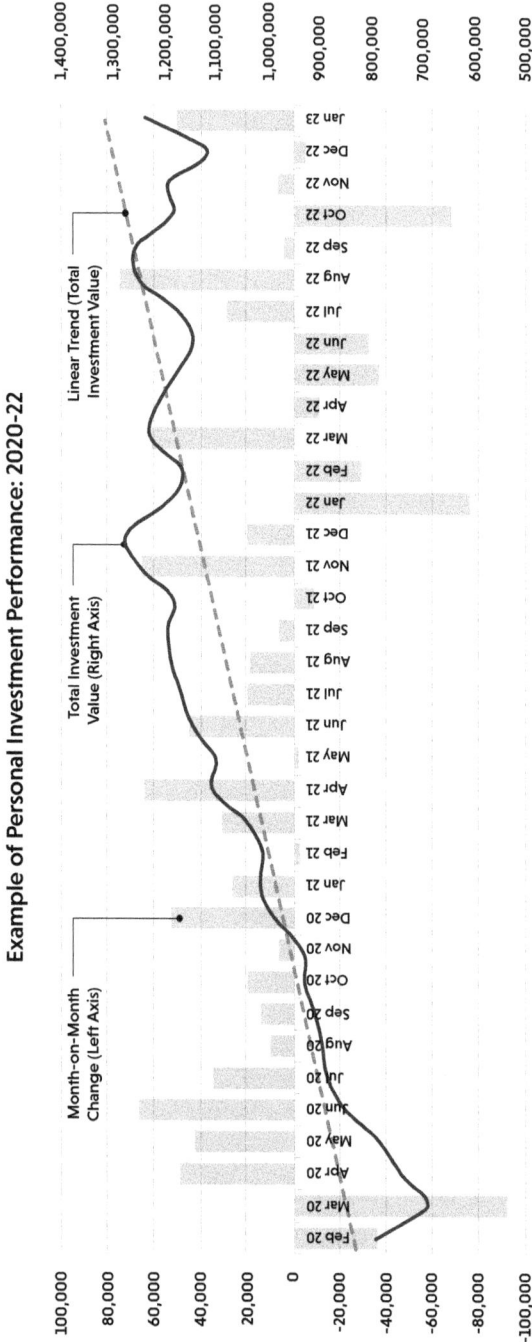

Example of Personal Investment Performance: 2020-22

Figure 12: Personal investment performance 2020 to 2022

I saw which investments were doing well and which ones tanked but still didn't have much of a strategy, even though I thought it was performing OK. This became the backbone of my pension and as I moved on from each job, I transferred the old company pension into my SIPP until it was a reasonable size. Because of this, I began to worry that I might not really know what I was doing, so I sought investment advice from a popular investment company. As part of this, they reviewed my portfolio performance and discussed the option of moving the management of my pension over to them. I was proud of my progress and the pot I'd amassed but felt rather deflated about the summary of my portfolio as 'rather eclectic' and found that it hadn't performed that well against several benchmarks. Nonetheless, I learned some important lessons from the review, the main ones being about duplication, dilution and trading costs. For the record, I took the discussion as valuable free advice and didn't transfer my pension. It's worth remembering that just because you're talking to a salesperson, you don't have to buy; if during the process you decide it's not right for you, you can always say no.

I invested in many different funds and one piece of analysis I received suggested breaking down the full list of underlying shares. This showed that some shares were held in several different funds, particularly the large global technology stocks. A large holding of a particular share wasn't a problem but holding shares in different funds was. For example, you might hold 1,000 Microsoft shares in two different funds but because of their different investment strategies, you might find one selling 100 shares one day while the other bought 100. At the end of the day, you still had the same number of shares but you'd been charged two dealing costs. This is another reason why investing in a single tracker is sensible, as it avoids this problem.

I had more than 6,000 different company shares in total (held in multiple funds) and we then focused on the smaller holdings or 'comet's tail' of the list. I remember L'Oreal as an example, because it transpired that I owned £300 of shares through one of my European funds. L'Oreal is a great company but what if it was so great that it doubled its share price? That would be a spectacular result for any stock but because my holding was so small, such an increase would only impact my portfolio by fractions of a per cent – so it wasn't worth it (no pun intended). Taking the example of the S&P 500 again, it covers 500 (big) stocks, so you're limiting your exposure to investing in many (very) small holdings.

Most funds and platforms are a little vague when it comes to transaction charges. Some are better at declaring the total monthly charge for managing your pension but how many transactions are happening each day in relation to your holdings? I didn't have a clue. Dealing costs are comparatively small but having no visibility of how many transactions you're making is a cost that's out of control. Against trackers, some 'buy and hold' funds will have significantly fewer transaction costs but the fee for the fund manager usually outweighs this. Similarly, large funds have a larger number of clients to spread the fees over, so costs can be lower. It's still not totally transparent but some of the tracking apps (discussed in Chapter 8) do pull this information through, which I find more helpful than trying to extract directly from a provider's website. It varies by platform but I can see transaction charges of around £100 a month for my investments and although I'd like them to be less, I'm reconciled to the fact that I do need to pay for the service they're providing.

Diversification

Next, let's look at diversification. There are two threads here – within your investments and for investments generally. Simply put, you don't want to put all your eggs in one basket, so it's a good idea to spread the risk. I've talked a lot about the S&P 500 and that's because it's a massive economy, hosting many major (but varied) global companies. The FTSE also lists many significant companies, so I do hold a couple of different trackers to give some geographical spread and, because I have a slightly adventurous streak, I also have some money invested in an emerging markets fund to capture some of the tiger economies of south-east Asia. Having such a spread is sensible but it's important not to get tempted to add just one more fund covering a slightly different sector because, before you know it, you're back to square one.

The second thread relates to liquidity, or how quickly you can convert your investments into cash. It's all well and good having a huge pension pot but not so good if you're unable to afford an emergency bill or cover a period of unemployment, so it's helpful to have a diverse range of investments and not all the same type. Pensions are straightforward as they're tied up until you're 55. ISAs are more readily able to be converted into cash and although you'd lose that year's tax-free benefit, it's not a deal breaker. Cash is obviously liquid in that it can be spent immediately but that depends on attractive interest rates being available. It's always good to have a cash buffer of 6 to 12 months' worth of general expenditure and my favourite way of doing this is through Premium Bonds. It's true that the 'interest' (prizes) isn't guaranteed but there's a fair chance of winning a prize (sometimes a big one) and statistically it's comparable with market rates so in my opinion, it's a better bet than the lottery.

The other common investment is property, or second properties and BTL. If you have a mortgage, it's likely to be your biggest investment, at least in the early years before your pension starts to accumulate. Shortly after getting married, we considered buying a rental property and took advice from my pension provider during an annual review. Their comment was that we already had a significant chunk of our potential wealth tied up in a property so would we be comfortable securing more debt, particularly as we were planning to move jobs and were a little unsure where we'd end up. This brought up the subject of liquidity and that it would be slow to release the capital out of a second house. It was through this discussion that we migrated towards a strategy of paying off our mortgage debt as quickly as possible over buying another property and equally contributing into both pension and ISAs. Having a quick look at our current spread, we have 50% in our pension, 38% in property, 10% in ISAs and 2% in cash and Premium Bonds. This isn't a specific target to aim for but it's a useful ratio to track once you've set up your plan. We haven't looked for the 'magic bullet' or utopian solution to investing but the approach we've taken to our spending and financial decisions has led us to the position we're in now.

Background research

I believe that several of the topics I've covered will be applicable and/or helpful to set you on a path on a better understanding of your finances, help you build a plan and have the confidence to make good decisions. But outside this book, where can you get more information or advice? Many investment platforms (for example, AJ Bell, Hargreaves Lansdown, Vanguard) provide interesting, unbiased and well-researched articles online, many with email bulletins. I'd suggest reading a range and picking the provider you prefer. I don't want to force you into reading the *Financial Times* every day (I certainly don't) but having some awareness of trends and movements in the markets is a good thing and it's going to be easier if you're comfortable with the way it's presented. Although more old fashioned, the traditional Sunday newspapers normally have a financial section that's not too heavy going and provides a reliable source of background information.

What I'd try to avoid are articles or posts that promote a share or investment tip with a catchy headline such as 'My inflation-resistant FTSE stock everyone should invest in'. It's far too tempting and, before you know it, you might be hooked on an extremely diversified portfolio – I know, I've been there. At Christmas, keep an eye out for financial journalists' stock tips for the year ahead and reviews of the previous year's predictions. If anything, it will underline that there's no such thing as a guaranteed investment. In all my years of reading these reports, I've never come across an article that reported 100% success.

There are also regular articles on poorly performing investments or 'dog funds'. Given that there are so many funds available and returns are variable, some are going to be at the bottom of the league table and there's always a selection of big brand names on the list. This doesn't really help you unless you happen to have an underperforming fund but the gist of my approach is not to major on managed funds but stick to low-cost trackers. However, it serves to underline the point that 'expert managers' aren't infallible. Even fund managers who have a sound investment strategy will have periods when the market goes against them – but don't jump ship after one poor set of results if you believe there's a sound basis behind the investment strategy and external factors that are impacting short-term performance can be overcome. Remember you're investing in the long term and don't try to time the market.

Where to invest and fee structures

We've touched on investment platforms, so let's address where and how you invest. If you're in a company scheme, you're stuck with their provider but when you're consolidating a number of old schemes or want to invest in your own SIPP, you need to choose a provider. Whichever one you choose, three things are important to consider: how much advice or support do you want, how big an investment range are you looking for, and what are the costs? You can usually find articles that rank platforms by cost but this isn't the only factor to consider; if you're comfortable making all your investment decisions, then the cheapest no-frills option could be the one that works for you. If you want a bit more support and advice, you'll have to pay for it.

Hargreaves Lansdown – a company I've been with for 25-plus years – are in the middle of the cost table. I can't recall why I chose them but they provide a usable interface, have particularly good supporting information and, while some argue their services are a little expensive, I can live with that because it's through their advice that I've built a significant pension pot. Without their content, I don't think my portfolio would be where it is today. I can invest in almost anything, which I like, despite it contributing to my highly eclectic portfolio!

While trying to rationalise my investments and migrating to simple trackers, I moved our ISAs over to Vanguard, a low-cost platform. I also transferred my last company pension as I wanted to trial their 'standard' pension package, given that I was nearing being able to draw from it and it felt right to be in a more structured fund. Both the tracker and pension (LifeStrategy 100% Equity) have performed well with low fees, which is a great result. The downside is that I can't invest in shares directly but the range of funds and trackers is great for a standard portfolio.

We've moved Lou's pension over to St James's Place, which is often cited as an expensive option and, by many, overpriced. They are also often the brunt of negative press articles. Given what I've written about the confidence in our financial decisions, this choice might surprise you but I can explain the logic. I often read on forums how easy it is to select and track your investments and how you'd be stupid to select one of the higher fee options, but pure investing is not the sole consideration, particularly as you approach your later years. After decades of self-investing, we hit the point where we were able to start drawing down from Lou's pension. While you can figure it out for yourself, we felt it was time to pay someone else to do the administration and give advice. We've also been impacted by both our mothers being diagnosed with dementia and the realisation that, despite our current confidence, at some point we'd need support in managing our finances. We felt it was time to engage with a financial advisor who we could get to know and develop a relationship with for the remainder of our investment time frame.

I listened to an interesting podcast discussing this very subject (TRAP 2023) – how much should you pay for advice? They used the analogy of going out for an anniversary or birthday meal. You'd want to go to a high-quality restaurant where the food was fabulous and you'd expect to pay a bit more for the experience. Therefore, when you're looking for financial advice, the question is do you want Michelin-star quality or Wetherspoons? Don't get me wrong, we love our local Wetherspoons and visit regularly – but not for special occasions! We'd hit a time in our investment cycle when we needed to have the support of a trusted advisor who could help with executing our retirement. Timing was key in our decision making – we'd been managing our portfolio perfectly well but knew we might not be able to in the future and took this decision to de-risk our later life.

When you start investing, the total fees are relatively small but they'll grow alongside your investments, so I'd suggest that, for the most part, you can replicate the basics of our low-cost model. But there will come a time when you want some advice and, if this is combined with a financial platform, you should mentally separate the fees from the pure management of your investments. Included in those fees could be a full financial health check every year, administration of our pension 'payroll' plus ad hoc advice ranging from capital gains (for example, selling a second property) to whether it's more tax efficient to spend from our ISA or withdraw more from the pension. We still have other investments in low-cost products but we can also tap into an advisor to help manage our plan as we get older. It was the right decision for us but there are many options and it's important to find a solution you're comfortable with. Not least, you have to be clear about your plans and aspirations and not accept a cookie cutter solution. We have a great relationship with our partner at St James's Place and regularly quiz her on all manner of financial questions, but most important is to find a solution or partner that you're comfortable with, and that you're getting value for money against what you need from them.

We researched three financial partners before making our choice and each had a different approach to fees. One quoted a straight 2.5% take-on fee to accept the portfolio, in addition to a regular management charge, which is a whopping £12,500 for a £500k pension pot. Another did a full financial analysis and cash flow modelling exercise as part of the pre-sales discussion, which was ours to keep (for free) and five years earlier had cost us £2,000. The final one didn't charge any take-on fee but there was a tie-in clause that would be payable if we left shortly after joining, on a reducing scale from 5% over a five-year period. Two quoted the sales gimmick, 'Our annual fees are usually 4% but for you, we've agreed 2.5%.' It's a big decision, not to be taken lightly, but beware of big fees. If you're starting from scratch, opening your first SIPP or ISA, there will be limited charges and fees will grow proportionally as your investment grows. The time to be cautious is when you've built up a reasonable pot and you're being asked to pay to transfer it somewhere else. Make sure you understand why you're moving and what you're getting in return. Yes, there are some costs involved in transferring investments and ultimately the recipient company is going to profit from your ongoing fees. I'm not a big fan of upfront costs to move but I understand such pricing structures are in place partly to offset the cost of pre-sales activity (ie advertising and spending time with you before you sign up).

Fee structures and transparency are an ongoing and contentious issue and there's no easy answer as to what's going to be right for you. However I'd go back to a previous theme of knowing exactly what you want, being comfortable with what you're being offered and whether it's right for you. For example, we had two criteria for moving some of our portfolio over to a paid-for service: one, would they handle the drawdown administration of Lou's pension and could they provide other, related investment advice; and two, did we like them and were they younger than us? Putting it bluntly, we didn't want them to retire or die before we did!

I've touched on financial advisors several times and it's right to consider them again. One piece of analysis they're likely to do (you can also find an online tool to do it for you) is related to your attitude to risk. Generally, it follows that bonds are lower risk (caveat some of my earlier comments) and shares are higher risk, so advisors will aim to match a portfolio to your appetite for risk.

Final thoughts

Our investment journey hasn't been perfect. We've made mistakes, losing money on some investments, so what I've learned is that it's important to recognise when to cut your losses and sell. It's the reverse of a concept called 'in for free' that a colleague and I used to use when we started investing in penny shares back in the 1990s. If we bought a share and it increased in value, we'd often sell our original stake, including fees, so we didn't make a loss but still had the residual invested 'for free'. Therefore we felt we had a pot of what was essentially free money and if another investment tanked and we lost the lot or had to sell at a big loss, we could offset this in our own minds against the 'free money' so we didn't feel so bad. It's OK to have an investment every so often that doesn't work out. There are many external factors at play, so just aim to be well informed and get out when you know you've lost and try not to repeat it too often.

I also acknowledge that we're not at the end of our financial journey and, while I don't tinker with my portfolio as much as I used to, I'm still tweaking what we invest in. Two years ago, we decided to differentiate our investments by different strategies to see which really is the best solution. Broadly we have:

- my ISA in a Vanguard World Index Tracker
- Lou's ISA in a Vanguard S&P 500 Tracker
- my original eclectic Hargreaves Lansdown portfolio

- Lou's pension with St James's Place, who manage her pension payroll and provide advice and have produced a portfolio based on Lou's risk profile and drawdown requirements
- my old company pension pots transferred into Vanguard LifeStrategy 100%
- a general investment fund (we ran out of pension and ISA opportunities) invested in 50% S&P 500, 30% FTSE 100 and 20% emerging markets (all trackers)
- Premium Bonds for our emergency cash fund.

As you'll see in a later chapter, the results are variable. They don't consistently track up and down with each other and have wide-ranging performance month on month. I even track the performance against key indices (World, S&P 500 & FTSE All-Share) and there's little correlation there either! Some months we beat the market, other times we're a little off and sometimes it's a mix across all of them. The only key trend is that overall, our portfolio value is slightly increasing. Which, given that we don't work, is a great result as it means we're withdrawing and spending less than the monthly investment returns.

There's an emerging trend to use artificial intelligence (AI) or 'robo-investing'. As technology has advanced, it was almost inevitable that at some point someone would use data and algorithms to replace the traditional fund manager to make investment decisions. These are now appearing as low-cost options to invest in, and in some cases, the results are good. However, it's too soon to be able to say whether they'll be able to deliver a consistent performance over five years, so at present, I'd still propose that the 'automated' tracker approach is best but I'll be watching this space with interest!

Key takeaways

→ When possible, make additional contributions to your workplace pension, particularly if your company will match them.

→ Fund managers can't guarantee performance and their results vary considerably. One exception is Warren Buffett, who famously showed trackers could yield better results, hence my strong preference for tracker funds.

→ Trace your old pensions and transfer them into a SIPP provider and either invest into their standard pension offering. If you're under 50 I'd go for the highest risk option (the percentage of shares/funds over bonds) as you potentially have another 15 years of returns to come.

→ Build up your rainy day fund (up to 12 months spending) in Premium Bonds.

→ Invest in your ISA; if pushed I'd suggest a low-cost tracker, either a world index or the S&P 500. At this stage go for accumulation funds over income.

→ If you can, drip-feed into your SIPP and ISA, even a small amount per month.

→ Track the value of your investments over at least a year and get comfortable with it going up and down in value.

Chapter 7

The elephants in the room

This chapter covers a few topics that aren't strictly related to investing and personal finance but will have a big impact on your plan. They are relationships, children and the sad fact that, sooner or later, we're going to die. I'll also revisit a theme touched on previously, that often we're not great at talking about some of these subjects, even to our closest friends and family. I can't stress how important it is to consider these issues when you start building your personal financial plan.

The first elephant I'd like to address refers to having kids – or rather, not having them. When we talk to people and they learn about our early retirement, they often comment 'Oh, well, that's because you don't have children.' I disagree that this is the sole reason for our comfortable financial position. Granted, it's had a big impact on the timing of our plan but it paints the picture that children are just an unavoidable money pit and that couldn't be further from the truth. If you have children, you have additional spending that affects your budget, but the principles of making spending decisions based on value still hold true. Similarly, while you might have less 'spare cash' when they're growing up, I'd still argue that the investment approach should be the same; it might just be on a longer timescale with smaller amounts. Estimates suggest (LV 2023) that the average cost of raising a child in 2023 from birth to 18 is around £200,000 in total, or £11,250 a year – and that's undeniably a lot of money. For that reason, it should also be part of your financial plan, as it's a commitment that you can't hand back. It's great to have a vision for your lifestyle in terms of house, car, kids, etc, but you can't escape the fact that realistically you need to have some sort of idea about how you're going to fund that lifestyle.

I'm not saying you have to be rich to have kids but if you choose to have them, you have an obligation to feed them, clothe them and bring them up in a loving and inspirational way so that they can make a positive contribution to society. If anything, you need to be more aware of your finances and your confidence in making sound decisions than someone who's single or child free. This book is based on our experiences and choices we've made but the endgame didn't start out as purely 'early retirement'; it just so happens that that was the outcome.

The starting point is to understand what you're spending on (why and what value you're getting from it) and having an idea of the lifestyle you want to lead as well as an estimate of what it might cost to fund. Next, review what you earn, proactively working towards regularly increasing that income, together perhaps with some smaller secondary incomes. Finally, put this into a plan that you can follow and keep on track, not forgetting that sometimes plans go off track. But if you know your plan and are able to manage the variables, you can get it back on the rails. When I worked for Amazon, there was a mantra, 'know the plan, nail the plan', and this sums it up well. Don't forget that this isn't a one-time effort; it's an approach to your finances that should see you through life and, if you have kids, to share it with them so they have sound expectations and the confidence to manage their own financial futures.

Having children shouldn't be an unknown in your financial plan. Yes, kids will increase your spending on the basics and may influence other high-value purchases such as cars or where you live, but it's better to build this into your thinking than not having a plan at all. It would be wrong of me to share any moral judgements on whether or not to have children, or how many, other than I believe it can be a great joy as well as a huge responsibility and it's a decision you (both of you, if you are not a single parent) should take ownership of.

Over the years, we've had friends and colleagues who have driven newer, more expensive cars, gone on more foreign holidays, had expensive hobbies like sailing or golf, always had the latest technology and subscriptions to the gym, Sky and Spotify – and many of them have children. In the main, they were, and are, 'making ends meet', so by understanding and reducing spending, there's scope for those savings to go into investments. Had we decided to have children, I believe our financial mindset would've been the same as it has been. Some of our choices may have been a little different and the timeline would have been longer but our approach to finances would've held fast because it emerged from the experiences we had and what we learned from them.

There's a cohort who might say that being restricted by such a plan is far too constraining and you should 'go with the flow' because you could get hit by a bus tomorrow. This is true but, in all likelihood, you won't – and you'll still have bills to pay. So while it might seem much more fun to be carefree, I can't highlight enough the benefits of having a plan to follow and, in particular, reducing your personal stress levels by knowing that you're in control of your finances. It may not feel like it when you start out but your wealth will grow incrementally as a result. Don't forget about the effect of compounding investment returns; if you start early, however small, your investments will increase over time and the approach we've taken can absolutely be followed if you have children.

Relationships and money

The concept of spending less, earning more and investing the difference works equally well whether you're single or in a relationship. If anything, it's a little easier if you're single as you're in total control of your financial decisions. Although Lou and I are closely aligned about what we spend on and how much, there are obviously some occasions when we disagree and one of us has to compromise. In many cases you'll be bouncing ideas off a partner – but if you don't have one, you can do this with a good friend instead. You don't have to be in a relationship with someone to mull over a big purchase. When I bought my first house, I spoke to my dad. When I was buying a car, I'd invariably talk to a mate – and usually took them with me on a test drive. When I needed some advice on a career move, I talked to my sister. It doesn't have to be the same person, either; I have a different approach to spending from my sister so wouldn't ask her about a new car but I would 100% trust her instinct with regard to my career. Being single is definitely not a barrier to having a sounding board for your financial plan. You'll have the same challenges as anyone finding someone you trust who's on the same financial wavelength as you and open to supporting you.

However, if you're in a relationship (or looking for one),

make sure you can talk openly to your partner about money. I believe it's fundamentally important to figure out whether you have similar attitudes to money. People are often labelled as being either a spender or a saver and you can see how opposing views might lead to problems if you don't agree on how your money should be managed. Although they say opposites attract, in this instance, I don't think it's a perfect pairing.

My upbringing influenced many of my beliefs and I'd expect it might be similar for you. My dad was the breadwinner and took all the big financial decisions while my mum stayed at home to look after us. They had separate bank accounts and a joint housekeeping account that Dad paid into but Mum managed all the household spending. I don't recall them ever talking to us about money or finances, other than my dad once explaining why he was in a bad mood when interest rates hit 15%. In later life, I started helping them with their finances by paying bills electronically and managing their bank account online, as they never really understood nor trusted the internet age. After Mum died and Dad became more frail, we had to have discussions about his care, which was hard to do, not least how much it might cost. Fortunately, Dad had an income from his (DB) pension, so he could afford care but he still refused to discuss his finances in front of Lou. I don't know why but there was a reluctance to talk about money and his view was that it was a subject for the men to discuss and not something to worry your wife with! Times have changed in terms of gender stereotypes but the reluctance to talk often remains.

Lou is tidy at home, a trait she adopted because her mum was so untidy. In a similar way, my parents' reservations about talking about money is probably the reason why I've taken an interest in sharing my knowledge. You should be having money discussions with your family – your parents, your partner or your children. It shouldn't be something to boast about or to be ashamed of but it's healthy to have open conversations about your finances in order to avoid getting into debt and making sure you have sufficient money to live on.

It goes without saying that you have to completely trust your partner – and this extends to finances. Throughout our 25-year relationship, Lou and I have had imbalances in our incomes but we've always split our investments between us, based on our joint financial plan. We invested equally in our ISAs and took advantage of personal tax breaks when I was a higher-rate tax payer and Lou wasn't. We've had a joint bank account since before we were married, as it seemed more effort to keep salaries and overheads going out of different accounts when we were already living together. Our view was that it was all 'our' money, irrespective of who earned it, and we made decisions jointly on what to do with it. This isn't for everyone and many of our friends have two personal accounts and one joint account but ultimately you enter marriage as a partnership for life, so why do you need to separate your finances? I know my view of marriage might be a little old fashioned, with the number of people in a legal partnership reducing and divorces rising, but I still maintain that it's unhealthy not to equalise assets and efforts in a relationship. Irrespective of how you term it, marriage, civil partnership or cohabiting, just be mindful and consistent in how you handle any joint accounts or shared investments and loans as you build your plan.

Divorce

Unfortunately, relationships can break down and when they do, it can have a significant impact on your finances – particularly if you're married or have children. Not only does it affect you after a split but money is a common cause of it. According to Divorce Online, the second most quoted reason for divorce in 2022 was 'the other party being bad with money'. In their blog, they cite that this is deemed a fault-based separation on the grounds of unreasonable behaviour 'that the other person is rubbish with money and/or general finances'. Examples of financial ineptitude included 'Racking up credit card bills, gambling, hiding money, buying expensive items that they could not afford and many, many more.'

I'm sure no one goes into a relationship expecting it to fail but tackling the question of finances early on would be a sound first step in determining whether or not you and your partner are aligned in your thinking. This needs to be both in terms of how you earn and spend as well as what your vision of your (financial) future looks like.

Whatever your personal situation – single, divorced, married, with or without kids – you can still follow the approach in this book. As I stated at the outset, everyone is different and therefore all your individual plans will vary but the underlying concepts remain consistent. And you never know, you may get hit by that metaphorical bus tomorrow. It might be cancer that shortens your life expectancy or a debilitating illness. And for that reason, just as it's important to talk about money, it's equally important to address the next big elephant in the room. At some point, we're all going to die.

We need to talk about dying

From my experience throughout life, as well as more recently while researching this book, if many of us seem to be a little cagey about talking about our finances, we're even more tight lipped when it comes to talking about death. It's likely that you've all had different experiences and that will influence how you think about this subject. My sister-in-law's grandparents are still alive, so my nephews are growing up knowing their great-grandparents, who still live at home, whereas both my parents went into residential care before they died and my in-laws are now in care. You may have had close members of family dying of an illness when they were young, or your only real experience is of older relatives dying of old age.

Either way, it will happen, and it triggers a number of important questions about finance, which is why I've raised it. Principally, if you need to go into care, it can be very expensive. This leads to the dilemma of wanting to have enough money to enjoy your retirement. You don't want to run out and at the same time, you want to hold some back in case you need to fund a care home. You might also want to leave an inheritance for your children.

Paperwork

First off, some administration – and something that came out of a financial review (with an advisor) we did about ten years ago. Make a will and consider a power of attorney (POA). Just the idea of writing a will when you're perhaps only halfway through your life can be daunting but important, particularly if you have children. There are often campaigns from charities or solicitors providing a free or reduced cost will-writing offer, so take advantage of that if you see one. Equally, be mindful about keeping it up to date, particularly if you have more children or change your relationship.

Dying without a will (intestate) can be challenging for those left behind, on top of dealing with grief, so please make a will. Probably the most meaningful impact of dying intestate would be how your inheritance is shared out, and it might not necessarily where you'd want it to go. This is particularly true if you're separated but not legally divorced (your ex-partner could inherit) or you're not in a legal relationship (ie living together) and your partner might not inherit.

A lasting power of attorney (LPA) is a legal document that allows someone to make decisions on your behalf if you're not mentally capable. Generally, this covers dementia but could be used if, for example, you suffered a head injury in a car crash. There are two types – one covering property and financial affairs, the other your health and welfare. I'd also suggest that, if your parents/guardians are still alive (or you have other elderly relatives), talk to them about an LPA, as it will enable you to help them as they get older. The risk of developing dementia increases with age (Dementia UK 2023), approximately doubling every five years after 65, with a one in six risk if you're over 80. It will be a difficult conversation, as most people don't want to relinquish control, or don't want to admit they might need some help. Either way, in our experience it's significantly easier to help an older relative when an LPA is in place, rather than trying to arrange it after they've lost mental capacity. Equally, you can help your family by having one in place too.

Funding your retirement

Before we get into the details of planning for old age, I want to address why this is important at an earlier stage of your life and where it fits into your plan. There's the traditional view of working life being akin to a hamster on a wheel – you work, get paid, you eventually retire at an age the government dictates, then you're given a State Pension that funds you through retirement until you die. It's no surprise that this was often referred to as 'being on the treadmill' – you just have to keep running, with no real control over your destination. However, few people now have a 'job for life' and the pension reforms of 2015 mean greater flexibility in terms of how and when you can access your accumulated pension.

Those reforms opened up a completely new challenge for pensioners – the fact that you can now manage your own (private) pension to fund your retirement, meaning you have a number of things to consider to make sure it lasts. Fortunately, the ethos of understanding your spending habits will help you here – but there's a tricky little subject to deal with and that's how long you think you might live. You don't have to manage it all yourself – you could just buy an annuity as described in Chapter 6 – but I believe you can get a better deal if you manage the drawdown yourself.

State Pension aside, for the majority of those with DC pensions, you now have this added choice of what to do with it – so you need to know how long you want it to last. For example, imagine you had a pension pot of £300k, wanted to retire at 60 and thought you'd probably not last beyond your 90th birthday. Ignoring any ongoing investment returns or inflation, you could take a tax-free lump sum of £75k (25%) and pay off the rest of your mortgage and perhaps buy a new car, leaving £225k for your retirement or £7,500 a year for the next 30 years. This is an extremely simplified case but it demonstrates the logic: £7,500 doesn't sound that much but you might also have some savings in an ISA, you might downsize and release some capital and, of course, you'll be able to claim the State Pension from your late sixties onwards (depending on when you were born and the prevailing legislation). Alternatively, you might have some underlying health conditions, no family history of long life and realistically don't think you'd make it past 80. Your £225k now only has to last 20 years or an increased potential annual spending of £11,250.

How long have you got?

The $64,000 question is, when will you die? As Brian Herbert wrote in his 2003 book *Dune: The Machine Crusade*, 'The only guarantee in death is its shocking unpredictability.' It's impossible to know exactly when you'll die but you can make some fairly sound assumptions from a combination of historical data and family history. The Office for National Statistics (ONS) reports from the 2021 Census that the average UK life expectancy (at birth) for men is 78.6 years and 82.6 for women. The ONS also provides a tool to show the probability of your death more accurately via their online life expectancy calculator. As a 52-year-old male, my life expectancy is 84, with a 25% chance I'll live to 92 and odds of 4.1% that I'll reach 100.

These are only averages, so it's helpful to consider your family history, as this will give you a better guide as to whether you're likely to be 'above or below' the average. Against my personal figure above, my parents died at 81 and 85, my two uncles in their sixties and while my grandmother reached 99 and my aunt died at 95, all my other relatives died much earlier, so (as a male) I'm comfortable with a 'planning age' of 85. I believe that's a little optimistic.

Having estimated the age at which you might die, you can now think about building this into your plan, as you have a time frame to work with. The reason for having your end of life in the plan is to provide you with a ballpark budget and also help you answer the question 'Do I have enough money to live on?' For this, we use similar maths as the example above but the inputs are annual spending and years: if you plan to retire at 60 and think you might live until 85, you've got 25 years. If we take the estimated retirement budget from an earlier example (£36k a year), you need to be aiming for an investment pot of around £900k. This isn't an exact figure;

it's to give you a guide and a target to work towards. If you take this approach and track your progress, you might find you hit that sweet spot earlier and can stop work at 58, or even 55. There are a few people who love their work and don't see it as a burden, particularly those who own their own business. Your partner might disagree, or at some point your physical or mental capacity might wane – so having a financial plan that you're tracking is still valid, if only to serve the purpose of knowing you're financially comfortable.

Back to your financial plan

Our idea to stop working crystallised around five years ago. We had taken to having a bath, a glass of wine and a chat on the last Sunday of every month, so it really was a 'eureka' moment! We were nearing completion on our small barn conversion and discussed what it might be worth. You could almost see the cogs whirring as Lou thought through her logic out loud. If our house is worth X (and we'll eventually move into the cottage) and you've got a pension worth Y and mine's worth Z, plus our ISAs, in total we have around £XYZ in assets. If you live to about the same age as your mum, then if we wanted to spend all that money, we'd need to be spending about £3,000 a month. At this point, we were both still working, had rental income and our monthly living expenses were about £2,000, so next came the crunch questions: 'What's the point of still working? Why don't we stop working and start spending?'

This was the beginning of formulating the plan to retire from work in our mid-fifties, to ensure it was achievable and not based on flawed assumptions. We undertook some financial analysis, specifically some in-depth cash flow modelling with a local financial advisor, and started talking about what our future expenditure would be in order to fund our proposed lifestyle. In a nutshell: what were our total assets and if we were to spend all the money by the time we thought we might be dead, would that cover our expected spending in retirement? Fortunately for us, whichever way we cut the numbers, the plan stacked up, so we took the leap of faith in 2021 to stop full-time employment and start our new lives.

Unless you have a quick and unexpected death (such as a fatal accident), you'll more than likely have a slower decline into old age, possibly compounded by illness or dementia, that will require an element of later life care. This is likely to be expensive but equally it will happen when your other discretionary spending will drop away, which will help to offset the cost.

Our base maths for retirement is simplistic but we did give some thought to how our spending might change over time. Our view was to broadly look at three decades. The first would include long-distance travel, enjoying quite a lot of socialising, going out and treats while we were still fit and healthy – and yes, it would be our most expensive decade. In the second decade, we'd reduce the travel or limit it to the UK and Europe and be slightly more sedate. We expect to slow up a little and not do quite so much but still enjoy a local social life. Similarly, our spending would reduce. Finally, in our third decade, we expect costs to rise as we buy additional care and support and, at some point, move into a smaller apartment or care facility. While costs will rise, downsizing will release capital and the State Pension will kick in. I admit this is a generalised view; we're using a flat monthly spending figure in our plan while recognising that it will vary but overall a single figure is easier to work with. The one unknown in our plan is our contention that we'd proactively move into a smaller retirement apartment or care home. Having witnessed this first hand with older relatives, the move is a difficult one to make and I understand why it's often not addressed. Such a move signifies an acceptance that your life is coming to an end and it also means giving up most of the physical possessions you've taken a lifetime to accumulate. It's also harder to do the older you get and why it's often left too late or becomes a distressing change.

Later life care costs

Looking at residential care homes (as opposed to assisted living apartments), data from the ONS and 2021 census suggests that typical life expectancy in a home for someone in the 70–80 age bracket would range from four to five years for men and five to six years for women. Partly due to this image of care homes heralding the final stages of your life, many people resist the move, preferring to 'soldier on' in their own property while everyday tasks become more difficult. Not least, your mobility suffers and with it, social interaction, leading to a downward spiral in your quality of life. Contrast this with having staff to cook, clean and look after you, as well as providing a regular range of social activities. Yes, it's expensive but you have pretty much everything covered and the only paperwork you need to worry about is the invoice. If you approach it with a positive attitude, you can have a comfortable and stress-free tail end to your life.

Our plan includes downsizing into more appropriate accommodation in our seventies. I hope we have the resolve to commit to that plan but know it's going to be a difficult decision. Either way, we've thought through the options. If you absolutely hate the idea of more support and care later in your life and want to stay in your family home and peacefully slip away in your favourite armchair, that's fine. Unfortunately, we don't get the luxury of choice but, as with other decisions, include it in your plan.

In terms of cost, average rates in 2022 (according to Age UK) for a residential care home were £800 a week and, if you require nursing care, £1,078 a week – although this varies geographically and by the quality of individual homes. These are big numbers: £41,600 and £56,056 per year respectively. Equally, the cost of additional care at home is expensive and can spiral upwards, without the benefits of a complete care home package, so while it's not guaranteed you'll need to spend it, it's better to be prepared for it.

There are many rules covering the funding of care but if you're reading this book, I'm making an assumption that you're interested in managing your financial future and you'd likely fall into the self-funding bracket. However, it's worth noting that when you look at care homes, there are options for some support. My point here is that you'd be better placed to research this earlier rather than dealing with it in your eighties when you're close to making some big life decisions. If you're looking for advice, engage someone accredited with the Society of Later Life Advisers (SOLLA), as they will have the most up to date information on options. If you have children, that's great – but don't automatically assume that they'll be on hand and willing to look after you!

Funding your core retirement

We've touched on what your final years might cost but what do you really need or want for your 'regular' retirement? It will obviously vary considerably depending on how lavish a life you intend to lead but, helpfully, there's frequently updated research that gives you a good guide. The table in Figure 2 (Chapter 2) shows figures of around £23k and £34k per annum for a single person and couple respectively (uplifted with a London weighting to around £28k and £41k). When we did our deep dive five years ago, our personal benchmark was £36k and we'd probably increase this figure to £40k given current inflation and cost of living headwinds.

Our approach is nominally to be 'broke at 85' but this rather flippant statement does need clarifying. We use it as a planning metric; if we were to spend all our money (less the value of our house as a proxy for living somewhere), at what rate would we need to spend it? We can then track against that figure to determine whether our investments are keeping pace with our plan or whether we're overspending against that plan. As we don't have children, we don't have the added pressure or desire to leave an inheritance. It doesn't mean that we don't have family beneficiaries in our wills; it's just that they'll receive the residual of our estate when we've gone, rather than specifying how much each of them will get. Depending on your circumstances, you may wish to set something aside or help family members financially while you're alive, which is fine, as long as you plan for it and don't leave yourself short. We also have a large safety margin in that we don't include the State Pension in our calculations, nor the value of the house, which realistically would be sold to fund a care home or assisted living costs.

It's also worth noting that investments can be treated differently after death and that should be part of your planning process. For example, you could retire at 60 and pay for a single annuity that pays you a certain amount each month for life. If you then die at 65, you may well have been paid less than the value of the annuity and, in this case, the provider takes the balance of that money. Albeit from beyond the grave, I'd personally feel cheated if this happened! If you have a SIPP, under current rules, since you still 'own' the pension pot, anything you don't draw down can be part of your estate to be inherited by your beneficiaries.

Summary

The endgame is to build an investment portfolio that covers your lifetime and is sufficient for your retirement at a time that suits you. While many people like think about 'the dream of early retirement', I'd contend that fewer people are prepared to consider and plan for the very real challenges they may face in later life, such as failing health and the cost of care. There are no hard and fast rules here and I'm not recommending a specific route other than to think and talk about what you believe are the best options for you, and build your plan accordingly. For the most part, I've promoted the idea of taking the long-term view, investing little and often, but starting early and not being too frivolous. As you get older, you'll likely hit a point when your mindset changes. For me, it was when my when my parents died but for Lou, it was after her cousin and a close friend were hit with stage four cancer diagnoses. Both died within two years. You suddenly think 'Hang on a minute, I could die tomorrow, so what's the point of saving? I should be spending and living for now.' For majority of our lives, we've followed the rather ambiguous concept of 'jam tomorrow' – or to paraphrase, don't spend it today, save it for tomorrow. But you'll hit a tipping point when you realise that you're beyond middle age and life is for living. The advantage of having taken the approach to 'save for a rainy day' is that, if you've invested sensibly, you now have the funds to do just that.

In the same way that paying off your mortgage lifts a huge burden from your shoulders, getting to that point in life where you can do pretty much whatever you want is hugely liberating. We retired early by following the principles laid out in this book and this has allowed us to do many things, not least to take time to look after our health, travel more and contribute to local community projects. We're much happier and healthier as a result. Acknowledging that not everyone will be able to replicate this entirely, I would hope that following some of the principles you can also achieve a more stable financial future than you might otherwise have had.

Key takeaways

→ Find someone you're comfortable talking to and broadly shares the same mindset.

→ Write a will and seriously consider LPAs for yourself and your older relatives.

→ Take time out to think about your whole lifespan. What might you want your retirement to be like, and where and how would you like to spend your 'twilight years'?

→ Take it slowly! This is a not a one-time exercise; it's about building your financial plan to a realistic time frame and meeting your needs.

Chapter 8

Managing and tracking your money

Now that I've outlined an approach to get your spending under control and reiterated the benefits of drip-feeding your investments in simple, low-cost products, how do you monitor it? I'm not going to suggest that you need to spend hours a month actively managing your portfolio but it's important to check it regularly with a light touch so you can see the progress you've made and whether you're on track.

There are two elements to successfully achieving this: knowing what your goal is and knowing what motivates you. In terms of your goal, it's great to have the 'big picture' idea of where you want to end up but you might also find it helpful to have smaller goals along the way. We didn't really think of our goal as 'early retirement' as some might understand it; we phrased it as being able to 'live comfortably without having to be tied down by earning a regular [employed] income'. This came about because we already had some rental income and knew the cost of our home and lifestyle, so we figured if we paid off the mortgage and had a reasonable pension pot, we could achieve it. It's not critical but it's a good idea to set a time frame alongside your goal to help you with tracking. For example, aiming to retire by the time you're 60 – but if it turns out to be 58 or 62, it's still a great result, so don't beat yourself up too much if you're a little off. This is about having a long-term vision, not a hard and fast deadline. Smaller staging goals might be to pay off your mortgage within 15 years, clear your credit card debt over the next four years or reduce your annual spending by 10% next year.

The second factor of what motivates you now comes into play. I've touched on motivation before and it's important in terms of how you track your finances too. I'm not going to give you a template and tell you which metrics to use, because if they're not your style, you won't buy into them. But I will suggest some that have worked well for us. For example, you might like the straightforward target of paying off your mortgage balance verses reducing your spending; both contribute to the same thing (spending less) but the mindset is different. Some of you will be happy looking at numbers regularly or plotting them on a graph, while others will be more engaged by the process and challenge of selling off unwanted items online and seeing the balance build up. Whatever you do, keep it simple! Although I do track several figures on a spreadsheet, it's not a complex one and it has now been replaced by the automated reports from an app. I probably overanalyse because I want to prove to myself that what I've stated is actually true; for example, as well as tracking monthly balances and month-on-month changes, I also look at a rolling six- and 12-month variance to smooth out any bumps or dips in performance – but you don't need to go into as much detail unless you want to. Whatever you do, don't worry – I'm not going to force you to spend hours in front of a screen puzzling over formulae!

Key metrics

The metric that we used most effectively is one described in an earlier chapter – and that's how much you'd need to spend to deplete all your investments by the time you die. In order to do this, you need to know:

- your net worth (the sum of all your investments, savings, ISAs, less any loans or debt) – explained in Chapter 2
- your life expectancy (the date you think you might die, or the later of the two if you're doing this with your partner)
- either your current cost of living or an estimate of the cost of living you'd like in retirement.

Simply take your net worth and divide it by the number of months you think you might have left to live. Compare it with your cost of living estimate and you'll see whether your financial position allows you to fund your aspirational lifestyle. I'm not going to lie – the first time you do this it will probably look dreadful and might be a negative figure but there's a reason why I like this metric to help visualise your financial health. First, if it's negative, it means you owe more than you've saved, so perhaps one of your mid-stage goals might be to turn this metric positive. Fortunately, every month, there are levers working to improve this ratio. If you're overpaying your mortgage, proactively reducing the balance owed and putting money into your pension, you'll be incrementally increasing the value of your investment. In addition, if you look at it every month, the denominator will have reduced (to put it bluntly, you've one month less to live and pay for).

Mortgage debt is likely to be the biggest reason for a

negative figure but the calculation can still be used if you don't have one and are renting. The difference will be that the future cost of living value will include ongoing rent, whereas this won't be a factor when you've paid off your mortgage. If you're renting but hope to buy in the future, don't try to build this into the calculation; just adjust the metric when it changes.

You might argue that you should include the value of your house or flat in your net worth and yes, while it's true that it's part of what you own, you still need somewhere to live, so you don't want to be including it in a calculation where you're literally 'spending everything'. Basically, this metric is just a simple snapshot of your current financial position, which ideally you'd want to track monthly. I (still) monitor ours on the first of every month and note it in a spreadsheet. It could look a little horrible for the first few months but once you have more than a year's worth of data, create a graph and you can more easily see your progress. As I've said before, there are no quick wins to wealth creation and the same is true here; it's unreasonable to expect immediate results. The beauty of this as a way to track your progress is that the ratio works in tandem with the 'spend less and earn more' concept.

Once you have this metric under way, you can then compare it to your target income and this allows you to answer the question as to whether or not you've reached the point at which you can retire, or however you've phrased your big-picture goal. Let's take the figure from Chapter 2 that suggests an annual income of £28,300 for a moderate lifestyle for a single person in London. This would give you a target of £2,358 a month and, in theory, if your metric was higher than this, your total investments (available to spend) would fund you for the rest of your expected life. It's simple but it works to give you clarity about where you are on the journey and when you'll achieve it. You can always change the target but the inputs should remain the same – only their values should change. You'll note I don't include the State Pension as future income, although in theory I should. I prefer to have it as my safety net and also as an additional hedge against inflation and increasing future costs. In essence, I'm pessimistic with this metric and it gives me confidence that if the numbers look good, I've still got some headroom in my plan to balance out any unforeseen future changes.

There are many other ways to evaluate whether you've saved enough for retirement but I'm not aware of an approach that helps you monitor how you're progressing in the way that this does. One approach that's worth mentioning is the '4% rule', not least because it's simple but it's good to have two metrics running in parallel because if both say you're doing OK, you probably are. The 4% rule is also referred to as the 'safe withdrawal rate'. Thinking of your investments, it's the amount you can withdraw each year without eroding your capital. If you'd amassed a pension and ISA pot of £450,000 when you hit retirement, you could withdraw 4% (£18,000) every year (or £1,500 a month) and the residual investment growth would retain a balance of the original £450,000. In essence, this is the reverse of some of the numbers shared earlier, that on average a stock market index will return a certain percentage and if you only withdraw that amount, your capital (original stock holding) retains the original value.

Taking the same figure and applying our 'broke at 80' logic, if you were 60 with a life expectancy of a further 20 years, you could spend £1,875 a month to deplete your funds. The two figures aren't miles apart and neither will be 100% accurate but they do give a good indicator of your long-term financial position.

It's true that both approaches don't take inflation into account, which will erode the spending power of your money over time. We originally tried to build in some investment returns and inflation into our model but when you start using average figures we tended to come out with the investment gains equalling out the inflation losses over the long term. That's why I'm comfortable using the flat figure analysis and not overcomplicating it by accounting for both inflation and returns. What the 4% model does help with is suggesting that you can spend from your investment while still retaining a balance, which is great if part of your plan is to leave an inheritance to others; it gives you a model for safe spending while preserving capital.

Some might argue that this analysis is too loose for such an important topic but, as I've said before, I'm not a maths wizard and needed something simple I could follow. It's also held true for us over the past 20 years, so I believe it has some credibility. What has also surprised us in our first 12 months is that despite our spending increasing and having no income, our net worth has remained stable and even increased a little against a backdrop of a not particularly positive economy. In other words, despite trying hard, over the past year, we've not been spending hard enough!

Technology and open banking

Tracking your investments might sound like a bit of a headache but advances in technology mean this is now much easier and the widespread adoption of open banking has further enhanced this. Basically, open banking is a mechanism that allows banks and financial institutions to share (customer and transaction) data via agreed interfaces with third party applications. Whereas in the past you had to rely on paper statements, you can now access your financial data from one consolidated platform as well as your bank's proprietary internet or mobile interface. Originally the main UK high street banks were asked to share data but as third party providers developed apps, more have followed and now most financial institutions share data to some degree. I've come across a couple of institutions that haven't yet integrated the technology but most of those have committed to it in the future.

What does this mean for you? Basically, less effort! In order to start spending less, you need to know what you're spending on and traditionally that meant wading through your paper statements or downloads. Now you can have an app that plugs into your bank and does it for you. And since it's (mainly) agnostic about which bank, you can easily combine multiple accounts in one app. They all work on a similar principle of asking you to log onto your bank or credit card within the app, which then pulls across any new transactions. Periodically, it will log in (effectively on your behalf) and refresh the data. As a safeguard, it will also ask you to re-authenticate the connection, typically every 90 days. Together with values, it also pulls across where the money is coming from or going to, which then allows the app to auto allocate into categories; either your income from work or spending on petrol, gym subscription, mortgage, etc. This makes it much easier to track your individual transactions, totals by category and your net worth, as well as spending and income trends. If you prefer, you can do it manually, but having done both, I'm in favour of using technology for this task.

You might be nervous about online fraud and the safety of other systems having access to your finances and you should obviously take proper precautions. Having observed the development of better security over the past five years, particularly with multi-factor authentication (MFA, where an additional confirmation via text, email or fingerprint is required for transactions), I'm confident that it's secure but it's good practice to be cautious. If anything, paying closer attention to your transactions might allow you to spot any fraud more quickly if you'd not really looked at your bank statements that closely in the past. Although it's an ever-changing challenge, I believe the bigger risk in terms of fraud is phishing – unwittingly giving over personal information via a call, email or message that allows crooks to replicate your identity, card numbers and validation credentials.

As to which app to use, there are several on the market; most do a similar job and each has its own style or niche. Examples are Emma, Snoop, HyperJar, Moneyhub and Monzo. Some are free or offer a free trial period and then either a subscription or access to additional functionality. Despite my love of 'free', just like fees on an investment platform, if you want a good service, it's not unreasonable to make a contribution. I've used three from the list above and settled on Moneyhub as a good all-rounder. It gives me what I need and I like the intuitive interface. However, this is more of a personal preference rather than a recommendation.

Note, however, that despite the slick interface and seamless integration, some data collection is a little clunky. Larger organisations share the base data of transactions cleanly and in full while others use a lower level approach, grabbing the data by virtually logging on and 'seeing' the transactions on screen. This works until the bank changes their layout and the screen-scrape technology needs to be recoded. This can lead to some delays or blips in the data but generally the issue is the connectivity with the target financial institution rather than the app. Fortunately, as standards are more widely adopted, this problem is reducing.

These apps are great for budgeting and auto allocating spending to categories, although it's worth taking some time to review these and not trust auto allocation carte blanche, particularly if you regularly buy from a big retailer across several different categories. You can buy homewares, groceries and garden plants from Tesco or Sainsbury's, so the allocation of your next £20 spend can be a bit of a lottery. That said, it's huge reduction in effort to grab all your financial data and the resulting spending/income trends and net worth analysis is invaluable.

Monitoring your data

When you first start tracking your investments, you're likely to get a shock one day when everything has suddenly dropped in value and you'll instinctively think you've made a mistake or taken a bad decision. Despite the fact that I look at ours every day, it might not be a great idea if you're prone to knee-jerk reactions. Investments go up and down daily and even though it's natural to be concerned when you see a drop, it usually isn't anything to worry about. It's the long-term trend you should be looking for.

To prove the point, Figure 13 (overleaf) shows our investments over the past 12 months. The solid black line represents the total value of pensions and ISAs, all invested in the stock market, some in managed funds but most in trackers. Some months are better than others and above average while others are not but the trend (dotted line) is still increasing. While we're investing a little each month into our ISAs, we're also drawing from Lou's pension. It took me a while to be comfortable with the drops but that came with looking at the data over a longer period of time and seeing for myself that the market does go up and down.

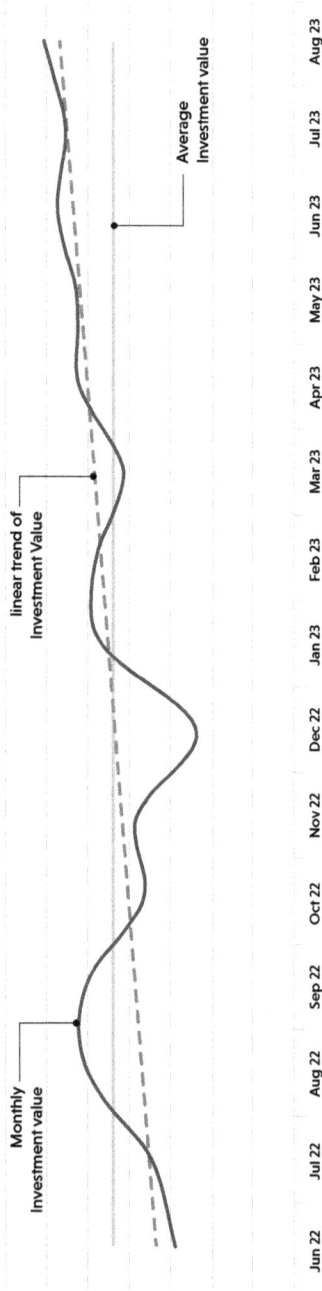

Personal Investment Value (Pensions & ISA): 2022-23

Figure 13: Personal investment value (pensions and ISA)

This is against a backdrop of a fairly weak UK economy but the returns are still positive. Having tracked my finances closely since university, it's been a similar story – much the same as the examples in the investment chapter showing that generally economies grow over the long term. This is despite some very challenging economic periods in terms of recession, wars, international terrorism, changes of government and, not least, Covid-19.

You don't need to go into as much detail as I do but, as part of my research, I started tracking our investments against three main indices – the S&P 500, the FTSE UK All-Share and the MCSI World Index. On the first of every month, I take their closing price and plot it alongside the spot valuation of our investments. In Figure 14, you can see that not only do the indices (bars) go up and down every month but they don't always move in tandem! Our personal investments are shown by the solid and dotted lines. We don't plan to beat the market – in fact, I don't think it's possible – but I'm comfortable that we're not massively losing against it on a regular basis. Think about it like this: if your investments have gone down 5% in a month but the main markets have lost 8%, you've done well. If your investments have gone up by 10%, how have they done against the main markets? I don't worry if I've not beaten all of them but I'm happy if I've done better (or 'lost less') than at least one of them on a regular basis.

Given the variable data in the graph, there's a note of caution when reviewing your portfolio or researching a particular investment. It comes back to marketing and noting that any investment fund will try to position their performance in the best possible light. While one might say they've performed better than a benchmark of their peers, another might show they've beaten a particular index or that their five-year returns are better than average. In other

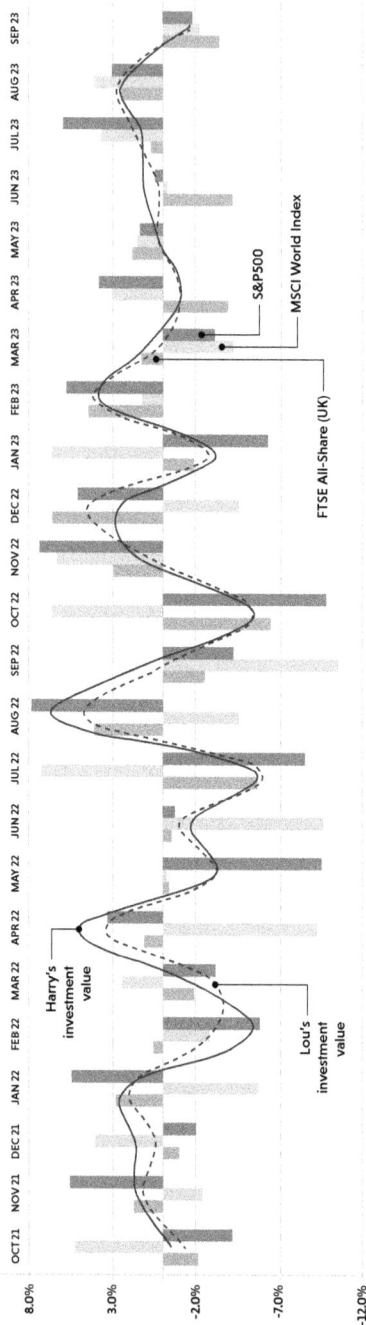

Figure 14: Personal investment month-on-month performance against main indices: S&P 500, FTSE All-Share and MCSI World Index

words, it's difficult to compare funds as their baseline is not a level playing field.

As detailed in Chapter 6, I like to look at fees, yield and the consistency of returns over five years, as well as the cumulative five-year performance. As a benchmark I then compare this with either the S&P 500 or World Index.

If you do talk to an advisor or someone proposing a particular investment, I suggest using the following two questions (loosely based on Warren Buffett's mindset) to help determine whether it's something to invest in:

1. How has the fund performed against the S&P 500 over the past five and ten years?
2. Do you believe the fund will outperform the S&P 500 over the next five years?

There's another common issue that stems from this regular volatility and arises when you transfer to a new provider. If you invest £50 a month over a number of years, you don't notice this volatility as much, partly due to the effects of pound cost averaging but also because you're actively increasing the amount invested. However, when you transfer a larger sum from one provider to another, if you hit one of those market falls, you see a quick loss in value. I often read posts on forums saying 'I've just transferred my pension over to ABC and it's dropped 12% in two months – should I ditch them?' My hunch would be no, as hopefully the market risk would have been explained before the transfer but mainly because I believe you really should give this sort of investment at least a year before making any rash decisions. It also depends on the fee structure of that transfer, and how (when) it is applied, but ultimately comes back to time *in* the market rather than trying to *time* the market. It underlines that selecting a platform or provider is important and you get the balance of fees and advice you're comfortable with.

Once you have an investment of a reasonable size, those fluctuations matter less. In other words, the bigger the investment pot, the less the impact. I look at our net worth figure daily (in part because it's on the front dashboard of Moneyhub) and it can go up or down by as much as £10,000 in a week but it doesn't worry me, as we're only withdrawing a tiny fraction of it every month and there are years of investment growth still to come. So provided it stays within a fairly broad range, there's no need to panic.

Therefore, building a larger investment pot protects you from market volatility. You don't need to be a maths wizard to do this – what you need is a basic understanding of finance and to follow the principles of regular investing in low-cost investments. The gist of this chapter is to show you how to manage your plan and feel comfortable with how it's progressing. There are no hard and fast rules for doing this other than finding a process that works for you and you can follow frequently and simply. When I was at Amazon, every team or project had weekly, monthly and quarterly business reviews (formally known as WBR, MBR and QBR) supported by a report or data, a discussion of the prior period and plans for the next. You don't have to be quite this structured other than scheduling a regular time to review your plan. Based on our eureka moment, Lou and I jokingly refer to our monthly chat as an MBR – our Monthly Bath Review.

Key takeaways

→ Choose what you want to monitor – either a single metric, a pure value or a selection.

→ Set yourself some targets and a timeline, together with a mechanism to track them that you're comfortable with.

→ Find time to review your progress regularly. It doesn't have to be weekly, possibly not monthly when you start, but I'd suggest a minimum of quarterly.

→ Don't worry if your metric goes the wrong way or your investments fall in value in a single month. What you're looking for is a long-term trend and being mindful of what the wider market is doing. The time to be concerned is when you're consistently trending against the major indices.

In a nutshell, what are you saying?

Chapter 9

Conclusions

I wrote this book in response to the many friends and colleagues who were intrigued as to how we were able to give up work at an age most would consider early for traditional retirement and how we were confident that our finances would support us. Working through how we'd actually achieved this, a close friend nailed it with the phrase 'spend less than you earn and invest the rest wisely'.

We then started looking at each of those three elements to understand how our approach might have been different from our peers'. Any references to products are purely based on our experiences and how they support the ethos of our financial lifestyle. We haven't been paid for any insertion in this book and you should be aware that there are often several alternative products available.

Spending less

In terms of spending, there were three parts. The first was the true cost of borrowing money and the principle of not being in debt, or clearing it as a number one priority. The second was that we didn't buy into the idea that many premium brands were great value for money; instead we made buying decisions on functionality rather than image. Third, we made things last, either through fixing them rather than replacing them, or simply not replacing them until they'd worn out.

If you have one, a mortgage will likely be your biggest loan and it's not just the headline interest rate you need to understand. How the balance is repaid is critical to ensure you minimise the amount of interest you pay. We believed in the idea of paying off your biggest debt as early as possible and this was our focus. We've had other loans and credit card debts and these were equally prioritised over any other spending after food and utilities.

Historically, some brands were, or felt like, a premium option and this was primarily driven by their low volume and therefore exclusivity, not to mention higher prices than mass-market options. Advances in technology, manufacturing and global supply chains have allowed many regular brands to now be of equal quality. The original Czechoslovakian Škoda was the butt of many jokes in my childhood due to cheap materials, inconsistent manufacture and poor quality, yet now it's a respected, high-quality brand. Indeed, when I chose mine as a company car, it was midway on this journey; I took a lot of flak but it was a very good, economical and reliable car. Similarly, the South Korean Kia currently offers the longest warranty of seven years and 100,000 miles, yet it's not yet thought of as a quality choice despite offering a better warranty than premium, more expensive brands.

The technical specification and features of products are often underused and therefore a waste of money when compared to the functionality you actually use. Take the compact digital camera; many have settings for different exposures, shutter speeds, filters, macro or night shooting, yet the default is the 'auto' mode, which most people stick to. We're living in an ever more commercialised world, driven in part by technological development. Marketing fuels this, enticing us to upgrade to a new version as soon as possible, or immediately our finance deal ends. If you can break out of this cycle, even by a few years, you can save money. It's also better environmentally.

Earning more

Again, this can be broken down into three parts: your career, your pension and what you can do alongside to earn something on top. Taking a proactive approach to your career will help you increase your earnings, with your skills, experience and attitude all areas open for consideration on how you might improve them. Whether you're employed full time, self-employed, contracting or part time, making yourself 'employable' will help you earn more or, more simplistically, offer something that someone else wants and is willing to pay you to provide.

Alongside employment, pensions deserve a special mention due to tax breaks and essentially 'free money.' Regular investments in your pension, however small, are your number two priority after paying down your debts.

There are several options to earn additional income, from selling unwanted items or leveraging cashback and loyalty programmes. Be wary of oversimplified media posts that claim to be a 'quick win', as I don't buy the idea of a shortcut for a reliable and guaranteed return. Property can be a profitable option for rental income but it's not open to all as there are high costs in buying property and the added risk from servicing the mortgage debt.

Investing

Financial investments can be complex and carry high risk, as you can't guarantee returns. This doesn't deter financial institutions from offering products or building funds that they believe will perform better than a competitor's. Some of these investments will generate returns but they come at a cost and there isn't a commercially created consistent performer.

What has proven to be consistent is the long-term reliable growth of equities. As such, a simple index tracker provides, in my view, the safest option for a low cost, diversified, lower-risk investment over ten, twenty or more years.

A final comment on investing and one tied to the primary objective of paying off your debts: however good an investment looks, never borrow to invest. There's always a risk, however small, that an investment fails, or more likely, doesn't perform well. There's too much at stake to take that risk.

What can you do?

Having read our story, you might be feeling a little overwhelmed and wondering how on earth you're going to do all of this. Fortunately, all of the elements are independent of each other, so you don't have to do everything, or do them all at once. You might already be driving a second-hand Škoda or be a great cook who enjoys preparing meals from scratch. Equally, some of the insights into investing or branding may be new to you and take some time to buy into. You can do as little or as much as you want or feel able to. Just by having a better insight how finance works may be sufficient for you, or that you start thinking about having a personal plan rather than drifting along and living life as it happens.

There's another element and that is personal choice, having the courage not to be influenced by peer pressure and being confident in your decisions. I chose to drive a five-year-old diesel Vauxhall Insignia and Lou a ten-year-old Ford Fiesta when colleagues were leasing a new Audis and Mercedes. Lou chose to wear a new pair of Dune boots from Vinted at half price when a friend bought a similar pair at full retail price. It was my choice to buy the previous model Android mobile when a close mate always has the latest iPhone on contract.

We have, of course, had some good fortune along the way – one being our marriage and finding a soulmate with the same ideals and mindset about money. Buying our house with some land was a bit of a gamble, not to mention a stretch on the mortgage, but securing planning permission was a step-change in being able to build a cottage to rent and cheaper than buying a second property. Some of our jobs have opened up opportunities for training and working abroad and allowed us to progress our careers. While we're not what you'd ever call athletic or particularly sporty, we have enjoyed good health. You may have different opportunities; you don't have to replicate ours.

Equally, it's not all been plain sailing and we've faced lots of financial challenges. Being made redundant and out of work for nearly a year; the gearbox failing on Lou's car and costing nearly £3,000 to fix just before we were planning to sell it; the oil tank splitting last year and needing replacement which, together with refilling with oil, cost £6,000 that year on top of the electricity bill.

I was chatting recently with a good friend who's spent her life in the nursing profession, with a particular interest in nutrition. While we discussed whether you really could oversimplify topics like these, we agreed that there were some analogies with the approach we've taken to that of dieting and weight loss. 'Spend less than you earn' is a similar concept to 'eat less and exercise more'. Of course, it's easy to say and harder to do; I'm still a little overweight and eat and drink a bit more than I should but it's the same approach to making it work. Understand the basics, set yourself a plan, monitor the results and find an approach that works for you. Just as you might hate the idea of going to the gym, you may find cycling a better alternative. The more you ride, the easier it becomes and you start to see the improvement in your stamina and distance.

It's the same with our finances. As we've progressed along our journey, we've been able to build in a buffer and have that 'rainy day' money that covered the unexpected expenses. The focus on spending on functionality, not brand, has also helped us to be avoid struggling to put food on the table or pay the bills. I know that we're fortunate to be in this position but it's the result of the way we've approached our spending and saving over many years. We also believe it's not rocket science and you could benefit too.

To summarise, below are my ten key points to help you gain money confidence for a more secure financial future:

1. Know what you're spending. Look at your bank statements and understand where all your money is going. Challenge yourself – do you really need to spend that much? It's not necessarily about cutting things out – it's about whether or not you're getting value for money and how much you'll use what you've bought.

2. Think about your job: what can you do to move up in your current company or gain skills that will get you a higher paid role elsewhere?

3. What can you do to generate some extra income or savings? Think about tax breaks, loyalty schemes or selling off things you don't need.

4. Don't ignore your pension. Enrol in your company scheme and find out where your old pensions are. Consider consolidating old ones into a SIPP in a simple tracker or packaged pension fund with low costs.

5. If you have a mortgage, understand the true cost and how much you're paying in interest. Focus on the rate at which the capital balance is repaid and aim to overpay.

6. Talk to friends or family. Try to overcome any awkwardness about financial conversations and never feel ashamed that you don't know as much as you think you should. You're likely to find that others are in the same boat.

7. Think about your retirement now. What would you like to do in later life? Understand what a plan to achieve this might look like.

8. Set aside some time on a regular basis (monthly is a good start) to check how your plan is doing. If you're confident with Excel, track it on a simple graph to better visualise your progress. Schedule a couple of annual tasks such as checking your State Pension forecast and your credit rating.

9. Don't get spooked if your plan wobbles a little. Understand that you're doing this for the long term and that blips will smooth out over time.

10. Don't forget to enjoy life. While extreme saving and frugal living is a way to build wealth, you also need to treat yourself once in a while – but don't let it become an expensive habit.

While it's a constant frustration for us to hear people say 'It's easy for you, you're rich', it's simply not true. Hopefully this book will dispel that idea and explain what our approach has been and how we've done it. I'm aware that there are other approaches to finance, particularly in relation to FIRE, building a BTL portfolio backed by mortgage debt, or the fees some investment platforms charge. Some of those views are expressed quite vocally on social media forums and vigorously defended when challenged. I'm happy with our approach as I know it has worked for us but accept that others may think differently. I'm not inclined to argue – just present our case and let the results speak for themselves. For those who do take a different approach, they're entitled to their thoughts and welcome to their views. In a couple of months' time, my view will be one of palm trees and blue sea in the Caribbean and I know which one I prefer.

I sincerely hope that some of the ideas in this book have resonated with you and will help you to start taking a few more confident steps to a more financially stable future.

Epilogue

Having completed my first book and re-reading through the final draft, I do understand that our financial freedom might feel like an impossible dream to many and that we were just plain lucky in what we've achieved. Thinking this through, I wanted to share where we were 20-odd years ago and have one last roll of the dice to persuade you that it's not impossible to change your approach to money and build your financial confidence for a more stable future.

Early in 2003, we were planning our wedding – there were lots of choices, discussions and decisions, not least as we were funding most of it ourselves. Of course we wanted it to be a special day but didn't have a huge amount to spend, and therefore made some untraditional choices. Unsurprisingly, we spent about a third of the average budget for a wedding at the time. We bought our wedding outfits in the closing down sale at a local department store (a £99 suit for me, a £90 dress for Lou). We were getting married in a small manor house, which was registered for marriages but also had a small chapel in the grounds for a ceremony and a marquee for a reception, so we negotiated a bulk rate at a local hotel for guests and hired a minibus for the day in place of the traditional wedding car. This meant none of our guests had to drive or had the hassle of finding a taxi.

We chose a navy (my suit) and gold/cream (Lou's dress) colour theme for our wedding and asked all guests to wear similar colours so that our photographs looked coordinated. We asked a friend to take three formal photos – one group picture with everyone, a close family one, and the pair of us with the cake. We also provided disposable cameras on tables to capture guests enjoying themselves. The photo on our mantlepiece is one taken by a relative, a candid shot of us walking into the reception. We decorated the reception with a bulk order of lilies (Lou's favourite) from the local florist and hired a helium canister for navy and gold balloons. Inflating balloons with helium the day before the wedding was one of the funniest times we've had and definitely got rid of any pre-wedding nerves.

We talked about the honeymoon and decided we could have a 'big holiday' at any time in the future, so instead we booked two £14 flights to Edinburgh and a five-star hotel for a week from a late bookings website at £100 a night. We didn't go to the Caribbean but we celebrated our 21st anniversary in Barbados – the first time for both of us.

We also got married on a Friday (cheaper than a Saturday), the day after the Iraq war broke out, when stock markets dived. We were lucky to have some financial gifts from family, which we invested and our first lesson in investment was seeing them rebound a few years later.

So although at times it feels like a lifetime, in reality 20 years ago we were just two fairly plain people with ordinary jobs and a large mortgage. We've talked and learned along the way, weren't too extravagant and made choices based on getting true value for money, making things last and continually drip-feeding whatever we could into investments. We've had our ups and downs but still found time for some fun along the way but with our own twist. Lou is fascinated by sharks, so for her 50th birthday we went on a shark-feeding day trip; not in some exotic location but at Birmingham Sea Life centre, followed by dinner with friends. Memories don't need to cost a fortune and you have to be willing to take bold decisions that might feel uncomfortable or against the accepted norm but financial freedom is achievable and worth it.

So now it's over to you. Good luck!

Resources

Introduction

Direct Line (5 January 2023) 'Less than a month to hardship for over six million households.' URL: directlinegroup. co.uk/en/news/brand-news/2023/05012022.

Marcus by Goldman Sachs and the Myers-Briggs Company (26 January 2021) 'What's your financial personality?' URL: marcus.com/us/en/resources/lifestyle/discover-your-financial-personality

Chapter 1

The Deming Institute '14 Points for Management.' URL: deming.org/explore/fourteen-points

Green, N (2023) 'What is a SERPS pension & can I cash it in?'. Hargreaves Lansdown. URL: unbiased.co.uk/ discover/pensions-retirement/managing-a-pension/ what-is-a-serps-pension

Chapter 2

Rowles, D (2020) 'The importance of diversification in volatile markets.'

URL: hl.co.uk/news/articles/archive/the-importance-of-diversification-in-volatile-markets

Websites to help you find a financial advisor:

- unbiased.co.uk
- ifa-direct.com
- fca.org.uk

Pensions and Lifetime Savings Association (2023). 'The detail: why do we need the standards?' URL: retirement livingstandards.org.uk/details

The Deming Institute: The PDSA Cycle. URL: deming.org/explore/pdsa

Vicki Robin and Joe Dominguez (1992) 'Your money or your life'. URL: yourmoneyoryourlife.com

Chapter 3

Martin Lewis, founder of consumer site MoneySavingExpert. URL: moneysavingexpert.com

Which? (2023) 'Food delivery apps charging double for some supermarket groceries'. URL: which.co.uk/news/article/food-delivery-apps-charging-double-for-some-supermarket-groceries-aaOVM1n9fD64

Houlton C (2023) 'Shoppers face double groceries cost when ordering from food delivery apps'. *Grocery Gazette*. URL: grocerygazette.co.uk/2023/06/05/cost-groceries-delivery-apps

Credit rating agencies: Experian and Clearscore. URLs: experian.com, clearscore.com

Mortgage calculator for online mortgage payment breakdown: mortgagecalculator.uk

Finance & Leasing Association (2023) 'Consumer car finance new business volumes fell by 6% in December 2022'. URL: fla.org.uk/media/news/consumer-car-finance-new-business-volumes-fell-by-6-in-december

UK Car Discount, online car broker: uk-car-discount.co.uk

National Car Finder, second-hand car auction broker and car sourcing service: nationalcarfinder.co.uk

Campbell, R (2022) 'Car pollution facts: from production to disposal, what impact do our cars have on the planet?'. *Auto Express*. URL: autoexpress.co.uk/sustainability/358628/car-pollution-production-disposal-what-impact-do-our-cars-have-planet

Ibbetson, C (2022) 'How confident are Britons in the kitchen?'. YouGov. URL: yougov.co.uk/society/articles/43386-how-confident-are-britons-kitchen?

Meal cooking packs: simplycook.com

Waste & Resources Action Programme (WRAP) (2017) 'Valuing our clothes: The cost of UK fashion'. URL: wrap.org.uk/resources/report/valuing-our-clothes-cost-uk-fashion

WRAP: action on food waste. URL: wrap.org.uk/taking-action/food-drink/actions/action-on-food-waste

Office for National Statistics (2023) 'Family spending in the UK – April 2021 to March 2022'. URL: ons.gov.uk/peoplepopulationandcommunity/personaland householdfinances/expenditure/bulletins/ family-spendingintheuk/april2021tomarch2022

Mosley, M (2021) 'How to cut food waste, help the planet, AND boost your health at the same time!'. *Daily Mail*. URL: dailymail.co.uk/health/article-10073963

Chapter 4

Dan White, spreading marketing ideas through illustrations: smartmarketing.me/illustrations.html

What Car (2022) '25 most unreliable cars'. URL: whatcar.com/news/25-most-unreliable-cars/n17550

Honest John Classics (2015) 'Top 10: 1970s company cars'. URL: classics.honestjohn.co.uk/top-10s/top-10-1970s-company-cars

Roberts, P (nd). 'Addicted to spending money: understanding compulsive shopping'. Priory Group. URL: priorygroup.com/blog/compulsive-shopping-and-spending-a-sign-of-shopping-addiction

Chapter 5

Amazon's leadership principles: amazon.jobs/content/en/our-workplace/leadership-principles

Vanguard (nd) 'When should you start saving for retirement?'. URL: investor.vanguard.com/investor-resources-education/retirement/savings-when-to-start

Institute for Fiscal Studies (2022) 'Green Budget 2022 – Chapter 4: Public spending, pay and pensions'. URL: ifs.org.uk/publications/public-spending-pay-and-pensions

Lontayao, R (2022) 'How much have UK property prices increased over the past 50 years?' *Mortgage Introducer*. URL:

mpamag.com/uk/mortgage-types/residential/how-much-have-uk-property-prices-increased-over-the-past-50-years/409501

Thrift +: thrift.plus/our-story

Gem Wholesale, trade wholesaler of retail clearance and returned products: gemwholesale.co.uk

Ferreira, C (2023) 'What is dropshipping and how does it work?

URL: shopify.com/blog/what-is-dropshipping

Chapter 6

Shaw, V (2023) 'Number of "Isa millionaires" surges to more than 4,000'. *The Independent*. URL:

independent.co.uk/news/uk/home-news/isa-millionaires-uk-business-b2385379.html

Diageo, example of shareholder profiles: diageo.com/en/investors/shareholder-centre/ordinary-shares/shareholder-profile

Adams, G (2022) 'Urgent warnings ignored and regulators asleep at the wheel: Growing fears that Gordon Brown's pensions timebomb may finally be about to explode.' *Daily Mail*. URL: dailymail.co.uk/news/ article-11317867l

Aviva (2023) 'What is pound cost averaging?'. URL: aviva. co.uk/investments/investing-for-beginners/what-is-pound-cost-averaging/

Maverick, J B (2023) 'S&P 500 average return.' Investopedia. URL: investopedia.com/ask/answers/042415/what-average-annual-return-sp-500.asp

Macro Trends, 'S&P 500 Index – 90 Year Historical Chart.' URL: macrotrends.net/2324/sp-500-historical-chart-data

TRAP (2023) 'We need to talk about SJP.' URL: youtube. com/watch?v=X_KpiFVQj3A (see especially from 37 minutes onwards).

Chapter 7

LV (2023) 'How much will it cost to raise a child in 2023?' URL: lv.com/life-insurance/articles/cost-of-raising-a-child

Keenan, M (2022) 'The 10 most common reasons couples get divorced.' Divorce Online. URL: divorce-online. co.uk/blog/reasons-for-divorce

Citizens Advice, 'Who can inherit if there is no will – the rules of intestacy.' URL: citizensadvice.org.uk/family/ death-and-wills/who-can-inherit-if-there-is-no-will-the-rules-of-intestacy

Age UK, 'Power of attorney.' URL: ageuk.org.uk/ information-advice/money-legal/legal-issues/ power-of-attorney

Dementia UK, 'How to reduce your risk of dementia or delay its impact.' URL: dementiauk.org/information-and-support/about-dementia/prevention-and-risk-factors

Office for National Statistics, 'Mortality in England and

Wales: past and projected trends in average lifespan.
URL
ons.gov.uk/peoplepopulationandcommunity/births-
deathsandmarriages/lifeexpectancies/articles/
mortalityinenglandandwales/pastandprojectedtrends
inaveragelifespan

Office for National Statistics life expectancy calculator: ons.
gov.uk/peoplepopulationandcommunity/health
andsocialcare/healthandlifeexpectancies/articles/
lifeexpectancycalculator/2019-06-07

Age UK, 'Paying for residential care'. URL:
ageuk.org.uk/information-advice/care/paying-for-care/
paying-for-a-care-home

SOLLA (Society of Later Life Advisors): societyoflaterlifead-
visers.co.uk

Acknowledgements

Like many first-time authors, I've learned there are so many things I didn't know, not least the actual writing but also the process of pulling it all together into what, I hope, you'll have found an interesting, entertaining and inspiring read. So my gratitude falls into two camps: first the inspiration behind the book, and then the mechanics of making it all happen.

A big thank you has to go to the many colleagues, peers and friends who simply asked the question 'How?' when they learned we were able to 'retire' in our 50s. This prompted me to think back on what we'd actually done and start writing down how we'd achieved it. At this stage, it was no more than a (very) big pile of notes and scribbled thoughts. It was a conversation with Sarah Megginson that gave me the final push and confidence to give it a go on the basis this wasn't just theory – we'd actually gone and done it. In turn, this led me to Beverley Glick to help me write and structure my words 'more better'. While at times it felt like being back at school handing in my homework, Beverley gave me the advice and guidance that I needed when I'd repeated something, contradicted myself or just waffled on too long along some random train of thought. It can be a challenge both giving and receiving constructive criticism, but our discussions were always good humoured and fair, and I believe it's much better read as a result. Equally, my thanks go to the whole team at the Right Book Company for their help and support in bringing this book together.

It goes without saying that my family and upbringing ultimately shaped my values, while friends, teachers and business mentors honed that view into how I now think about life, and in the context of money, evaluating and making decisions. Additionally, I owe a debt to those managers who supported and trusted me to mentor junior colleagues, and opened my eyes to the rewards of simply helping others find their paths through their varied opportunities and lives.

My biggest thanks will always be to my wife and soulmate, who has not only been part of this journey for more than 25 years, but supported and challenged me, making it a team effort to have got to where we are now. As she will openly admit, before we met, she'd given little thought to pensions and financial planning, so she became my sounding board for building our finances, and a reality check when approaching financial decisions. Like the book says, we talked about money.

EU Safety Representative: euComply OÜ Pärnu mnt 139b-14 11317 Tallinn
Estonia hello@eucompliancepartner.com +33 756 90241